Buried Secrets

Anecdotes of a Funeral Director

Harry Pope

Buried Secrets: Anecdotes of a Funeral Director
This print edition published in 2018 by
AG Books
www.agbooks.co.uk

AG Books is an imprint of
Andrews UK Limited
www.andrewsuk.com

Contents

Setting the Scene. 1

My Early Days 5

My Last Year with This Firm 18

The Middle Years 26

Traditions, Tales, and Strange Occurrences. 43

KAT. 52

Epilogue 99

Buried Secrets

Setting the Scene

A nationally represented funeral company had a van converted to a private ambulance. It had room for four bodies to be securely strapped to stretchers in the rear so no staff had to ride in the back. The vehicle stopped on a steep Croydon hill, one of the stretchers was not as secure as it should have been, and the forward motion meant that it suddenly and with force hit the rear doors.

Body and stretcher landed on the road, doors wide open, as the private ambulance drove off.

Much gesticulating from anxious pedestrians, a lot of horn blowing from other vehicles. The driver pretty quickly realised what had occurred, reversed back with the assistance of his colleague riding up front, they retrieved their load, and continued back to the depot.

Nothing more would have been said, but the two men found great humour from the situation, recounting to their colleagues back at the garage. The incident soon found its way to management, an inquiry was held, and while the two men had a black mark against their records, no further discipline ensued.

These days, in the very unlikely possibility that it would even happen, the men would be so contrite, ashamed, they would report the incident and await their fate, safe in the knowledge that it would have been captured on a phone and already on social media. They just would not get away with it.

This book is set in the period between 1977 and 1992, when the funeral business atmosphere was very different from today. The funeral profession was a male preserve, with women only allowed to serve the role as funeral arranger, nothing hands-on, not allowed to be involved where any physical contact was necessary. That was because ladies were deemed too delicate to have to involve themselves in lifting anything heavy.

Of course, when men get together, they usually have a bizarre sense of humour, and this book reflects the amusing situations of the period. That's not to say that nothing funny occurs today, it's just that the standards of professionalism are far higher today, and that some of the incidents in the early days of this book were tolerated as letting off steam, just men working together, whereas today they are regarded as unacceptable.

A prime example involved a south London competitor in 1979. The two men had been to the hospital, collected the body, and were returning to the yard about five miles away. They were on overtime at an hourly rate, so decided to pop into the cafe for a bacon sandwich and a mug of tea. The Transit van with body inside were left unattended for about half an hour, and when they returned the van, and body, were gone.

It had been left in an area known for casual car crime, and it's safe to assume that the miscreants had no idea as to the contents, just stealing a reasonably new Ford van. The van was missing for two days, while the funeral company managed to avoid informing the family that their relative, albeit once safely in their care, at present, strictly speaking, wasn't.

The Police were frantically looking, while of course being amused at the predicament, and it was retrieved, abandoned, two days later, with no-one the wiser. The point I make, though, was that the two men were disciplined, but not dismissed. That was the late 1970s, it certainly would not have been tolerated in this day and age. Corporate responsibility, and what is socially acceptable, have considerably improved.

To continue setting the scene, also bear in mind the funeral business scenario that was to be transformed. The vast majority of businesses were smaller family run enterprises, had been in the same family for generations, being passed from father to son. There might be a monopoly in a particular large-sized town, but nationally only two or three companies were that big.

That was to change, with the advent of mergers, acquisitions, and pure greed on the part of one particular individual, who will be mentioned later on in this book. No, don't go peeking, or you will miss memorable moments.

It was the end of the period where gentlemen were funeral directors. They were no longer called undertakers, that was considered a passé word, they wanted the respectability of the newer title. Professional standards were improving, so the staff education had to improve as well.

A manual was written by a very well respected funeral principal called Thomas Hands Ebbutt, a Croydon man following in the family tradition. This covered all aspects, so then an examination was set, so standards could be achieved. All to achieve respectability, but it was still a closed profession for newcomers. If you wanted to succeed, you had to work for a larger company, gain your Diploma, be a good person, and when you were 65, allowed to retire, usually on a more than generous final salary pension.

No new businesses were allowed to be created, for one simple reason. The death rate was in the region of 610,000 annually, and the existing companies could not create any more business. Therefore, any new business would take business away from the existing ones. Start-ups were actively discouraged.

The only way for a funeral business to grow was to acquire an existing one.

There was a lot of complacency at the time, with the local family businesses believing that because they provided the local service, to the local community, living where they worked, knowing their clientele, it had always worked in the past, so it would continue. But financial institutions were looking at the overall picture, realising that costs could be reduced by buying out a lot of smaller companies and spreading the overheads.

It is easy to forget that there are three main areas of financial outlay for funeral directors. Staff. Vehicles. Premises.

All of these would be reduced by dissemination. And the vast majority of smaller companies owned the freehold of their properties, a lot with shops on the ground floor and tied management accommodation above. Staff were kept happy this way through reduced rents in exchange for out of hours telephone and office duties.

By the time I started as a chauffeur bearer in 1977 the whole industry was ready for a major overhaul, but in my lowly role of that I was completely unaware.

My Early Days

Little realising at the time, I was very fortunate to live close to one of the best family run funeral companies in Sutton, Surrey. They really were a good company to learn with, and those three years proved to be a very good grounding and experience.

At the time, they had six local offices, with a central garage. I was allocated an Austin Princess limousine, registration MLD 6D. Strange the things you remember, but it was a pig of a vehicle. Just like all the other limousines I have driven over the years, it was impractical, uncomfortable for the driver, and a fridge in winter while an oven in summer. Very few had air conditioning, they all had shiny leather seats where you had to hang onto the steering wheel when negotiating any kind of bend as you would slide away from the controls.

There was a sliding glass partition to separate chauffeur from passengers, which was always kept shut so passengers could be candid about the deceased in private. The back seat was uncomfortable, room for three alongside each other, reclining at a slight angle. Between the partition and the back seat were fold-down collapsible seats for another three passengers, quite an upright seating position, and on one memorable occasion I had to execute an emergency stop. The three heads behind me on the occasional seats went bang bang bang onto the glass.

It had a four speed manual transmission, with the gear lever on the steering column. Reverse was next to first, and the worn gate meant that it was very easy to select the wrong initial direction. Potentially embarrassing. The gear change was so slow that if you were on anything other than a flat or downward incline, first gear was impractical to use, because momentum was completely lost between first and second gears.

I hated that Austin Princess limousine, and on one memorable occasion the daily garage orders read "HARRY IN GARAGE ALL DAY TO CLEAN AND POLISH HIS LIMOUSINE". It's a wonder that they continued to employ me, but I suppose they saw something worthwhile in me. All day my limousine was parked at the back of the garage while my colleagues went about their daily duties. All my labours were directed into ensuring that the limousine was restored to the perfect pristine condition shared by the other vehicles. At the end of the day it was inspected by management, with a grudging nod of approval. As my superior went by, he muttered 'about bloody time.' Without knowing it, my reputation for maintaining a clean vehicle was poor.

On my first day as a chauffeur bearer, I carried a coffin for the first time. When I was getting ready for bed that night, my wife looked at the area around my neck and shoulder. 'What's that love bite doing there?' No, I hadn't been caught out doing naughties, it was the weight of the coffin nipping the blood vessel. At least, that's what I told her.

I am under 5'7" tall, and when a coffin is carried am in the corner that is technically referred to as the sharp end. The other end is referred to as the blunt end. Easy to distinguish, because one is wider than the other, simply because the shape of a body means that the shoulders are wider than the feet. The upper end of a torso is heavier than the foot, so as I am smaller, would usually carry on the lighter foot end. That always goes first, so the taller men, at the back, have a more even distribution of weight.

There was a hearse driver called Keith, who had an evil sense of humour. We were the same height, so usually were paired on the foot. When the coffin is carried into church, the conductor, or man in charge, follows behind the priest, then the coffin, then the mourners. As the coffin is on the men's shoulders, their hands can't be seen. Professionals don't raise their hands and hold the coffin, the weight is sufficient to carry the momentum.

We were going into a country church for the service, followed by interment in the churchyard. It was a narrow aisle, and the pews were almost brushing our thighs as we were carrying through. We were still a little short of the waiting trestles at the altar, no one could see what was occurring, when I was suddenly aware of Keith's hand wandering over to mine. But his hand didn't stop there. It proceeded to play with my testicles. Gently but firmly.

I had to pretend that I was sucking a lemon to prevent showing my face. My first reaction was to burst out laughing, impossible, so all I could do was look at the floor as I placed the coffin on the trestles, and filed past the mourners waiting in the doorway. Keith had a large bruise on his shoulder after I told him my feelings.

***

A few months later, it was wintertime, and we were interring in a country churchyard. It was one of those days that bearers dreaded, pouring with rain, soggy underfoot, a long carry from church to the grave which was right at the back of the churchyard, uneven path, difficult underfoot, and a heavy coffin.

Three very large and heavy floral tributes on the top of the coffin, a very uncomfortable experience for the men carrying the coffin. You knew that your raincoats were going to be saturated, you knew that they weren't sufficiently waterproof to avoid your suit under it being soaked, and as for the polish on your shoes, there was no way that they were going to hold their shine, as they were covered in mud. The occasion was one of deep mourning, and as it was one of the older churchyards the grave was a narrow one, with other older ones either side. This one was re-opened, but still quite deep. In the usual way, the gravedigger would make the sides even all the way to the bottom, a level surface, then wooden boards around the top to prevent the sides from giving way, and grass matting on top to make it look pretty.

The gravediggers forgot the wooden boards. And I had to stand on the section that had the weakest edge.

We placed the webbing through the handles, and started lowering into the grave after the nod from the vicar. The natural weight took the webbing through our fingers, but because of the rain, the sides started going. With me at the weakest point. First my feet, and then my legs, slowly slid into the grave, with the weight of the coffin on top of my torso. I became wedged, half in, half out, of the grave. Pouring rain, three colleagues starting to laugh at my predicament. So did the conductor. So did the priest. So did the mourners. Suddenly it wasn't quite such a solemn occasion, and it took my three colleagues at least half a minute to get round to doing something about extricating me.

More bruising when I undressed that night.

***

The owner of the company was referred to as 'guv'nor' by all the garage staff. It's an endearing way to refer to the boss, and one he encouraged. He had two sons, both in their twenties at that time, and the guv'nor was the third generation funeral director.

He rarely went out in charge of the funeral, content to let his staff be in control. Sometimes he would attend as a mourner, occasionally even when they were only casual acquaintances. The traditional funeral companies had a very good policy of assisting each other with the training of their offspring, who would ultimately inherit the business, and it was very common practice for the son in his late teenage years, instead of attending any higher education establishment, to work and live at a competitor who would be some miles away. Excellent grounding, also establishing relationships that would live on for many years to come.

Each of our firm's male principals had a garage driver allocated to chauffeur them when out in the evening, and the guv'nor had one of the senior men who had been with him for many years. The eldest son came into the business after I had been in the garage for a couple of years, we hit it off as there was an age disparity of a few years, and I soon became his driver.

But before that, when I had been in the garage for about six months, I had my first accident. Well, it was serious to me, and extremely embarrassing.

Any purpose built limousine is a very long vehicle. Usually twenty feet, it is also wide, to accommodate six passengers in the back, and there is an overhang from the back bodywork to accommodate the large boot. This extra bodywork can catch out the unwary, as there is another four feet behind the back wheel, and when reversing the mirrors don't show at all clearly.

I had dropped the family off at their house after the funeral, on my own without the funeral director who had other duties to perform elsewhere, so was trusted to remember where they lived. Unfortunately, this was in a cul-de-sac, and they were almost at the end, by the turn round area. I swung round outside their house, opened the door, let them out, and had to execute a three point turn, as the circle on the limousine was terrible. They had just arrived at their front door when there was a terrible noise. Metal on metal.

My rear bumper had met a lamp post.

We all examined the back of the limousine. They were very sympathetic, tutting as they examined the huge dent in the middle of the metal bumper. We then looked at the lamp post. Nothing. Very sheepish, still with my chauffeur's hat on my head, I drive away, back to the garage to admit my inability to reverse.

The garage was empty as I reversed in, dark at the back, so maybe I could have tried to get away with it, but that wasn't the company ethic. Through the back door as I exited my limousine came the guv'nor and Stuart the garage mechanic. I immediately went up to the boss and said

'really sorry guv'nor, but I have to admit to you that I've dented my bumper.'

They both looked at it, looked at each other, and the guv'nor said 'f***ing idiot'. He was renowned for his ripe language.

He turned to Stuart and said 'you can fix that, can't you?'

'Yes guv'nor'.

'That's all right, then. We'll say no more about it.'

I learned a lot from that incident. How to gain the respect of your employees.

***

People can die at the most inconvenient times of the night, and an example occurred when a gentleman passed away at 3am.

The authorities were called, with the appropriate steps completed. It was clear for the phone call to be made to the funeral company, so within an hour or so the two men on duty were woken from their slumbers to go to the house to collect the gentleman. His family preferred him to be taken to the chapel of rest rather than wait for the next morning, so the duty staff were pleased to be paid the standard three hours overtime, despite it taking less than an hour from the time they received the phone call waking them up and returning to their still warm bed.

He was an elderly married gentleman, the couple living in accommodation connected to their son's house. The son of the deceased was a very caring man, and despite being devastated at his loss, also had to be very considerate to his elderly mother. She had taken her husband's demise quite well, probably being prepared, as her husband had been receiving hospital treatment for some time.

He had arranged everything, and it was the son who knocked on the front door of the funeral director's premises at 7.30 the next morning, asking to see his father. A very unusual request, so not unreasonably, he was asked 'why?' His reply was quite simple. When father had been taken away during the night, his false teeth had been handed to the staff to accompany, so he could be ultimately prepared for his final journey.

The problem was that mother, despite her grief, was wanting some kind of normality, and that included breakfast. She could not eat any meals, because her false teeth were accompanying father, and they needed to be swapped before she could eat the first meal of the day.

Discreetly, the swap was accomplished.

***

Fortunately for this book, others have been able to contribute, and I am grateful to David Thompson, a past company general manager, for the next reminisce.

This would have been in the early-1970s, in his first year. The scene was Bandon Hill Cemetery, in Wallington, Surrey, a horrid winter's day, burial ground exposed on a hill to the elements, and it had been snowing.

Rain, snow, they are both as hazardous to the bearer with a heavy load on his shoulders. David had the unfortunate physical size to be one of the taller men, so always carried on the head end, with the extra weight.

Bandon Hill was one of the newer cemeteries, council owned and run, with a grim superintendent who had a persistent glower, living in a house located just inside the cemetery gates, and a short walk to the pub where he spent most of his evenings. His assistant might in the early days have shown some sense of humour, but by the time I was acquainted with these two gentlemen any laughter lines on his face had been replaced with a dour countenance.

The superintendent was only a few months older than his deputy, so the unfortunate underling knew that his only prospect of an early redemption was his boss occupying the designated at present empty burial plot that was awaiting his final resting place.

The cemetery chapel was a couple of hundred yards inside the gates, and it was the custom for the superintendent to await the arrival of the cortege, and then walk with the vicar and the funeral director to the chapel doors. Normally, the procedure was to then replace the coffin into the back of the hearse for the drive to the grave, which was usually some way away, as it was a very large cemetery. David and the rest of the crew were in for a bad day, however.

While the service was occurring, there was fresh snow on top of the previous ice, so it was impossible for the hearse to drive the short distance to the grave. Nothing for it, the men had to have the coffin on their shoulders, being really careful how they walked. But they could only shoulder so far, the last few yards had to be carried in hand.

That is because of gravestones in the way, too narrow to negotiate easily, so the four men would be manoeuvring the coffin very gingerly over the ice, gravestones, ruts, to the open waiting grave. As it snowed.

David's feet slid.

He tried to save the situation, but impossible. He decided to save his fingers instead, because there's nothing like a coffin landing on your hand to provide maximum pain. The coffin was sturdy, no damage there, but as it went down, David landing on top, there was only the floral tribute on top to save his face from the impact against unyielding and unforgiving wood. It was mimosa arranged in a metal frame.

Facial impact against this object meant that his glasses were knocked off his face, his nose bleeding, and as well as the floral impression on his face, the mimosa was impacted and had to be gently removed.

The widow was very kind, providing David with a hanky to stem the bloody nose. She also gently removed the mimosa, with no scar remaining to this day to mar his otherwise handsome features.

He remembers little of the rest of the day, as there was slight concussion. We were hardy in those days.

***

The people coming into the funeral profession these days have many advantages over us older ones, more training, more learning, more qualifications, but something I have over the lot of them is the fact that I had on the job training, learning as I went along, and there was one incident from the late 1970s that they will never see. I can guarantee that they will never be involved with a gypsy funeral as I am just about to describe.

I was a lowly, ordinary limousine driver, one of six on this funeral, where we arrived in a country lane in the depths of the Surrey countryside. It was a gypsy caravan site, one designated as a site for permanent residence, with probably up to a hundred people living there. The patriarch had died, and it was to be a huge affair, with travellers arriving from all over the country, as well as Ireland, to pay their respects.

Flowers for travellers' funerals are always elaborate, with the prestige of spending more than anyone else on your tribute. In those days there was a particular florist that didn't advertise, didn't have a shop, but made floral arrangements just for the travelling community for all occasions. I have no idea if they are still going, you won't be able to find out for yourself, as they receive instructions via word of mouth. Strictly cash, they don't pay tax I am sure, they are there to provide a service for a specific area of the community, you will never even know their contact details, they are so secretive.

But their arrangements are simply the best, bespoke to instructions. I have seen: three square feet cricket pitches with full teams that needed four men to carry so it didn't break: boxing rings with ropes, two fighters, referee, seconds, red flowers depicting blood on the floor: huge horses, with rider, all on a metal frame; a caravan to scale complete with a man in traditional gypsy costume sitting atop. These tributes would take a normal florist days to complete, supposing they would agree to the commission in the first place. But this particular florist would have a team on standby, ready to accept every single order so it could be complete for the funeral in a few days time.

I seem to recall that they had a week on this occasion, they must have worked late into every evening before they had all ready. When we arrived at the site, we were greeted with a good couple of hundred people milling around, three flat bed lorries, and more flowers than I could possibly count. The whole day had been allocated for this funeral, our crew were there just for them. It was a warm spring day, so our first task was to very carefully load the flowers onto the lorries, saving the family tributes for the hearses. We had two, a horse drawn one for the coffin, and the second just for flowers.

It was mid-day before we arrived at the church, with a long cortege following the two hearses, flat bed lorries, limousines, and then family vehicles. Following tradition, they carried the coffin into the little country church, which had already been decked with many flowers. A lot of alcohol had already been consumed that day, so those conveying the coffin into church had a more difficult task, with a very unsteady progression before none too gently deposit onto the trestles before the altar.

Doors were left open throughout the service, with a steady stream of men quietly leaving to find a tall tree to hide behind while conducting their business. While the service was going on all the funeral men were taking as many floral tributes as possible to the graveside, with some of them having to be handled very carefully due to size and potential to break up during transportation. Hasty repairs were not uncommon in these circumstances.

We had just about finished sweating with the tributes when the procession exited the church with the suited male mourners attempting to make their way between the gravestones. Country churchyards are notorious for hiding hazards for the unwary coffin bearer, so these men had a particularly problematic duty as they were feeling the alcoholic effects as well as the need to relieve their bladders. As main mourners they had been unable to make subtle exits. Soon they were beside the grave, with the professionals threading the webbing though the handles ready for lowering. Very soon the minister was intoning the words of interment as the weight of the coffin took him down very fast to the bottom of the grave. They stepped back, we stepped forward, took the webbing away, so the gravedigger could pass them the five spades. All men took it in turn to back fill, but it still took them over half an hour of continuous labour to complete. One male mourner removed his hat, which was then passed round to be filled with cash for the gravediggers

It was then time for hugs all round, back in the vehicles, for the return journey to their site. And this is where the uniqueness of the occasion occurred for me. The limousines were instructed to park in the narrow road outside, and we were not allowed to leave. We were told to come onto the site and watch the final part. Intrigued, we stood on the fringes as the patriarch's wooden caravan was wheeled forward. It was gaily freshly painted in red and yellow patterns, and the main male mourners poured some petrol from cans onto it. They then set the caravan alight.

It soon went up, complete with all his possessions.

This was the only time I ever witnessed a traditional traveller's funeral with the burning of the family caravan. It just doesn't occur these days, those new to the funeral profession over the last thirty years will never see the likes again.

The next day the family went into the funeral office to pay the account in cash. No questions were ever asked as to the source of this huge amount, but the manageress was sufficiently foolish to hand over a receipt, and place the cash in a drawer for paying in the bank later in the day.

Half an hour later when she went into the drawer it was empty.

***

We had a lovely garage mechanic called Stuart. He had the responsibility of maintaining the ageing fleet, which he just about managed to do. He was also on the duty roster, so if someone passed away outside normal business hours two men earned overtime by collecting the body and removing to either the public mortuary on behalf of the coroner, or back to the chapel of rest.

Stuart was a blusterer, you might have heard the expression bullshit baffles brains. That sums him up, and he would often attempt to fog a situation he didn't comprehend himself so you couldn't realise his lack of knowledge. Stuart ultimately rose to the challenge of self-employment, starting his own funeral business which proved to be very successful. He sadly passed away before he was able to appreciate the fruits of his success, and his son Howard has more than proved himself to improve the foundations.

He was usually rostered to partner Ralph, the garage foreman, a figure of authority who had favourites. These were allocated the cushier jobs, able to disappear for long periods during the day to spend refreshment time while their colleagues were in the blinding snow, or sweltering in their hot vehicles.

This particular incident was all the sweeter to the rest of the garage staff, because it involved these two gentlemen.

7pm on a summer Sunday evening was the time, and the location was the Roundshaw Estate. This is sprawling, on the site of the old Croydon aerodrome, and where problem families were inserted amongst people who had pride in their surroundings. Very little crime, the place was kept clean and tidy, flowers, anti-social behaviour was frowned on, and you knew that if you had a funeral from the estate it was impeccable, with a tip for the men at the end.

Stuart and Ralph parked the private ambulance close to the bottom of the steps leading to the flat where the deceased was waiting, they took the stretcher into the flat, and despite the weight managed to carry back downstairs without incident. They placed the stretcher on the back of the ambulance, closed the doors, Stuart got behind the wheel, and they looked at each other.

'Have you got the keys?'

'No, I thought you had them.'

'No, you're the driver, you're responsible for them.'

'well where are they then?'

Their attention was drawn to outside the vehicle, where three local Roundshaw youths were sitting on their bikes, doing nothing, just staring at the front of the private ambulance. They were close to a drain.

Stuart and Ralph then realised that these three lads were smiling. Grinning. Then openly laughing. Because the ringleader had the ignition keys in his hand. Staring straight at Stuart the driver, he opened his fingers, slowly releasing the bunch. They didn't just land in the gutter, down they went into the drain, never to be seen again.

**

My duty partner was a man called Len. He used to drive the hearse, I drove a limousine. It should have been the other way, so he would have been Lennie the lim and I would have been Harry the Hearse, like two characters from Damon Runyon.

A strange thing, really, but a lot of funeral staff failed to make old bones. Stuart and Ralph passed away at early ages from heart problems, as did Len. A lot suffer from back problems in later life, as I do, because of the weakness caused by carrying heavy dead weights.

However, Len was one of those characters you go through life and never forget. The funeral profession is full of them. He had no tact at all, swore constantly, and didn't ever realise how offensive his language could be. One lunch time in the driver's mess room, Len was holding forth about something close to his heart, maybe like fishing, and after five minutes I interrupted him.

'Len, do you know how many times you said the word f***in the last five minutes?'

The room fell silent. 'I'll tell you, It was 84.'

'I f***ing never!'

Because of his lack of tact, on our first weekend together I wanted to gain first hand experience from an old hand what to say to the recently bereaved. It was 2pm on a hot Saturday afternoon in August, and we had to attend a house in close to one of our country branches. The procedure was to bring the body back to head office and be placed in refrigerated conditions for the weekend.

The poor lady had been looking after her infirm husband for a long time, so the death was expected, though sudden, as she had been out shopping, returning to find he had sadly gone. Doctor called, happy for us to come and collect, we placed him on the stretcher, so Len and I went back to reassure the lady that he was in good care, and answer any questions she may have.

Widow. 'Thank you so much for taking care of my husband. Where are you taking him to now?'

Len 'Back to our head office, madam'.

Widow. 'Oh, I thought he would be going to your local office.'

Len. 'No, they haven't got any fridges, and he'll go off over the weekend.'

My Last Year with This Firm

Len was a lovely fellow, but completely unsuited to speaking to the public, It had been discreetly suggested to me by management that I speak to families whenever possible, short of barging him out the way. By the time of this incident, it was 1979, and we were duty partners of long standing.

Fawlty Towers was a very popular programme, and there were no such thing as video recorders. It was transmitted on BBC2 at 9pm on a Monday night, and this particular evening Len and I were on duty to respond if a body needed removing. The phone went at 8.30pm, so I knew I was going to miss my favourite half hour of laughter. I quickly went upstairs at home to change, and Len and I were outside the house by five to nine, ready to collect the deceased.

Len was driving as usual, I knocked on the door, and it slowly creaked open. Unlocked. Light on inside, a voice called 'we're upstairs.'

I slowly went upstairs, bedroom door ajar, inside were two policemen. The lady was lying in bed, chest of drawers at the foot, with a large telly on top. The two coppers were seated alongside, just waiting for us to turn up. Our role was to transfer the lady from her bed to the public mortuary, claim a standard three hours overtime, and miss the programme. However, I surveyed the situation, and asked the two policemen

'Are you in any hurry?'

'What do you mean?'

'When are you supposed to finish your shift?'

'Ten.'

'So it wouldn't be a problem if the removal took a little longer than expected, say if we hadn't been here until 9.30?'

'Nope, what have you got in mind?'

'Well, Fawlty Towers is on in one minute, and we're all going to miss it. But we don't have to...'

They looked at each other.

'It's okay with us if it's okay with you.'

I went downstairs, and called out for Len to join me. Bemused, he came to the door, and I informed him that we were going to watch Fawlty Towers, and then complete our task. Len said

'What about the coppers?'

'They don't want to miss it either.'

So for the next half hour, there was the bedroom, with two policemen one side of the bed, the two undertakers the other, the body in the bed, and the four of us watching her t.v. End of programme, we turned it off, took her away, the two policemen secured the house, and no-one was any the wiser.

What had we done wrong? We didn't hurt anyone. We didn't claim for extra overtime. We just behaved like any normal blokes, with discretion. And which episode was it? No, not the one with the body in the hotel where the guest died suddenly.

***

One of the staff, Don, had started as a 14 year old boy, working in the coffin workshop. This was way before WW2, and in those days the firm had even owned their own forest, providing sufficient timber to keep the supply of coffins going. These days, with so little oak and so much cremation, the quality is nowhere near the same.

It was nothing for men to work for the same company for fifty years, man and boy, and for the company to look after them when retired. If sufficiently fit they would usually return to work part time, offering their experience for the younger men. On reflection, it was strange how much influence these men had, and were referred to for opinion when required. This is a custom that has all but disappeared, but in the late 1970s there were four or five of such men, who were always there in the background, and I frequently found myself among this old crew. I learned a lot from them, and I regard it as a shame that this fund of experience and knowledge is no longer available in the funeral profession. Big business has overtaken the smaller family run one, and it's not necessarily a good thing. Yes, they can work alongside each other, but it's something of an uneasy alliance.

Don was old school, always immaculate, and by the time I worked under him he was the head conductor. He could have been the general manager of the company, but he was content in his role, seeing out his days in this way.

The firm had their own workshop, as well as their own subsidiary company that made the coffin linings. My wife's Auntie Joan, who was 100 on Christmas Eve 2016, was a contemporary of quite a few of these men, living in the same back streets of Sutton, attending the same school, playing together as kids, sometimes even marrying.

Auntie Joan was working in the lining factory when Don came in one day. He was a dapper man, a glint in his eye for the ladies despite many years of marriage, head of white hair, well trimmed moustache, top hat always brushed, no hairs on his collar, nor any dandruff. The owner of this ancillary business was also a school contemporary, so Don came in to tell him his tale of woe.

A bereaved lady, while on a funeral, had stepped away from the coffin, which was being attended to by Don and the crew. Don had carefully placed his umbrella and top hat nearby, as they were in the way while he supervised the handling of the coffin. Lady client wasn't looking where she was going, and stepped onto the top hat on the ground.

She was wearing high heels.

Don brought the hat in with a huge hole in the top, wondering if it were possible to repair in the workshop. He was somewhat aggrieved that despite all the skills at their disposal, they were unable to return it to its pristine condition.

To make matters worse, he had a complete sense of humour by-pass when the group of workers, led by the director in charge, continued to laugh until he could stand no more and left the building.

***

This comes under the section of 'You Couldn't Make It Up.'

There is a very wealthy residential area to the south of Croydon in Surrey called Coulsdon, and as previously mentioned the company have a branch there. One of the largest houses in the wealthiest area was owned by a gentleman in the City of London, and he passed away. In those days it was frequently the custom to take the body into the house the day before the funeral so the family could pay their last respects to the deceased. This was especially common with families who had originated in Ireland.

The money associated with this house was phenomenal. There were five large quality cars parked outside in the gravel driveway, and still room for the hearse and two limousines. They must have had a permanent gardener, because the grounds at the rear were also extensive. It was a matter of prestige that the send off should be lavish, but in good taste, so he was brought home to the top floor the evening before and placed in his master bedroom.

The day of the funeral was to involve a Requiem Mass at the local Catholic Church, followed by burial in a new grave at a local churchyard, so no expense had been spared. The service in church was to start at 10am, so we were at the house at nine, as a lot was involved at the house. There were a lot of floral tributes, so my role with two other men was to bring them from the house to the hearse. Four other colleagues went into the house with the conductor to seal the casket and bring it downstairs.

Inside the house, it was a scene of subtle luxury in extremely good taste. The entrance hall behind the front door was large, with many rooms leading off, the lounge enjoying panoramic views of the extensive grounds. The wooden floor had a couple of quality rugs, a major trip hazard for those carrying a coffin, as the rug would easily slide. The men were made aware by the conductor.

The staircase was wide and sweeping, dividing half way up so bedrooms could be accessed from either side. The entrance to the stairs from the vestibule area was in the middle, to the right at the bottom of the staircase was a large well polished oak table, and to the left was a man in a black suit, white shirt, black tie, playing a white grand piano.

There were six bedrooms, with the coffin waiting for the men in the master one to the left. There was a wide landing between the top of the staircase and the bedroom doors, with wooden balustrades. On the matching corners were two large ornate also wooden urns, filled with a variety of seasonal flowers.

I saw nothing of what occurred, but was told in graphic detail afterwards. The casket was a heavy 14 gauge metal one, a flat lid, and three huge floral tributes adorning the top. This meant that there was a considerable weight, because he had been a tall heavy man in life with huge appetites. It had been an early demise but a full life. Four strong men will still struggle to cope with these demands, and because the landing was wide, and staircase long and sweeping, it was decided that there was sufficient room to manoeuvre if the men carried the casket on their shoulders, even going downstairs in this way. Usually, this would been a sensible decision, bearing in mind the sensitivity of the occasion, with many people watching and the tinkling strains of Beethoven being played on a white grand piano at the bottom of the stairs.

The conductor went first, walking backwards, so he could take the strain of the casket as it went down stairs. Completely normal, but unfortunately, and I wonder if you have guessed what's coming, his elbow stuck out. There was an urn in the way. Full of seasonal flowers. Something had to give, and it was the urn. It came crashing down, to the bottom of the stairs.

If the fates had been shining on him that morning, if he had got out of bed the correct side, if the children had got ready for school uncomplainingly, if his wife had kissed him as she handed him his sandwiches with a 'have a nice day, dear', then the urn would have broken on the floor, lots of apologies, yes a red face, but nothing more. But no, the aim of the urn was cruel, and landed right in the middle of the grand piano. The white one, playing Beethoven.

The music stopped.

Conversation ceased.

Nothing for it, all the men could do was continue carrying the casket downstairs, placed it in the back of the hearse, and the conductor had a very embarrassing few moments conversation with the family before they left the house.

***

I won't reveal this person's identity, but one of the conductors was unpopular with the staff. That was because he was known to keep some of the tip money for himself. His system was quite straightforward.

When you are the person in charge of a funeral, you have a certain uniform. That involves, during the summer, wearing a top hat, a black tailcoat, waistcoat, white shirt, discreet black tie, striped trousers, and well polished black shoes over black socks. During winter an overcoat was substituted for the tailcoat. The waistcoat had four pockets, two lower, two above. His subterfuge was simple.

In the top two pockets, he would have two five pound notes. The bottom two pockets were empty, so when at the end of the funeral the satisfied chief mourner wanted to give a thank you to the men, he would place the note, if more than £5, in one of the bottom pockets. The £5 would then be produced as testimony to the client's satisfaction, keeping the larger one for himself.

He maintained this subterfuge for many years, and only stopped when he realised that the men were onto him. The next thing he did was to still have the £5 notes, but every time would place the higher value note behind the £5 in the same pocket, bringing out the £5 as proof.

The only staff to share in the tip box were the garage and coffin workshop, and it was administered by a committee of four, including Ralph the foreman. Records were kept as to the success of each conductor, the man in charge, and it had been an open secret for many years that this man was keeping something for himself, such was the disparity between his figures and the others.

It was decided that matters had gone too far, so he was taken to the back of the garage after work one evening when most had gone home. Some of the men pointed out to him that he was going to receive a pasting if he didn't see the error of his ways. He did.

***

David Thompson provided me with the next anecdote. It concerned Ralph the foreman.

He was a strange character, when I started he hadn't been doing the job for very long, inheriting it from his father in law, who had worked for the firm for fifty years, retired, and returned on a part-time basis. Ralph was still growing into the job, which involved being in charge of the men, collating overtime, ensuring that they were clean and tidy, and supervising the collection of bodies from hospitals and nursing home.

He was very popular with the nursing home staff, having a very pleasant way with the ladies. He could be obdurate with the men, often making unpopular decisions that went with the job. I do not recall that he had a subtle sense of humour more taking pleasure from the discomfort of others. However, this tale shows that indeed he did have the ability to be funny.

David and Ralph had to attend a removal of a very unfortunate lady who had passed away while smoking a cigarette in her bed. She had been enjoying a glass of whisky as she was reading a romantic novel, and it's safe to assume that she fell asleep while reading. The cigarette continued to burn, and she passed away due to smoke inhalation, which in my day frequently occurred and was the cause of death in surprisingly frequent instances. The Police had been called, and were present until the two men arrived to take the old lady to the public mortuary, where cause of death would be established. Policemen are particularly squeamish when it comes to touching people who have passed away, so it was up to Ralph to examine her for anything of value, which would be noted and returned to relatives later. This is a straightforward procedure, one that we were all very used to. Ralph took the eiderdown back slightly, and dictated to the copper the rings. He then gently removed the eiderdown, and something fell to the floor. Ralph said to the policeman

'Write this down'.

Pencil poised over notebook, Ralph dictated

'One Alsatian burnt down to a Pekingese.'

The Middle Years

At the time I was ambitious, over thirty, one failed business before coming to the funeral profession, and wanting to make a success of my life. There was one problem with this. Dead Men's Shoes.

Promotion was not on merit, but length of service. Loyalty was the great key to success, and if progress was to be made, then I had to wait my turn. Two men had joined in the five year period before me and been promoted into the office, no vacancies there. Ralph was firmly ensconced in his role of garage foreman. There was a deputy foreman. Stuart was in charge of vehicles. The prospect for promotion was bleak, I was going to be stuck in the same job for many years to come, there was only one way to progress, and that was outside the company.

My first employers are in a South London borough, and six or seven miles away in Croydon is a well established company but in a somewhat moribund state in 1980 because of inept ownership and management.

The funeral family had owned the firm since its inception, but due to financial mismanagement found themselves in a position unable to defend against a merger with a larger South London company about ten miles away. There were six Croydon branches, mainly profitable, with a Croydon garage/depot in the Old Town close to the by-pass and flyover. As with other businesses, they owned the freehold of their premises.

The area manager was an impecunious family member, in charge of the Croydon area head office, close to site of the long gone the old variety Davis Theatre, under the new-ish fly-over. It had its own small car park at the back, room for six cars parked considerately, he had his own office with his wife working in the main general office.

This is where the workers sat. We were tolerated because we were paid a small wage to keep us happy, while earning the firm their profits. The two juniors were Martin and myself, with the lovely Tina as telephonist and also funeral arranger when required. There had been an advert in the Croydon Advertiser for an experienced funeral director, but the quality of applicants had been poor. Despite the fact that I had never arranged a funeral previously, never been in charge, I was taken on.

The nemesis was my boss's father.

He and his wife lived in a remote country office where they were well known in the community and could do little harm. Their front office was used for funeral arranging, and he had two sons. I never met the younger one, who had worked for the firm but left under a cloud some years previously. There were rumours, but I never asked too much. My boss's father had his own office, which he mainly used for falling asleep in the afternoon.

The atmosphere in the main general office changed every afternoon about 4pm when father arrived back from his long lunch at the Conservative Club. He had always driven back in his company car, always over the legal alcoholic level, but we were too cowed to do anything about it. All funerals that had been arranged during the day had to be presented to him.

The paperwork would be waiting on his desk, he would return, light up his pipe, and puff away as he went through details. You were then summoned into his office to reply to his barked questions, the paperwork would either be torn up in front of you, or he would simply draw a line through. A tough learning process for a newcomer to the business. These days it would be regarded as bullying and a reason for constructive dismissal, but this man's influence was so great that no-one would ever get a job with a different company within a ten mile radius, and even then would be fortunate to find a lowly under position. What am I saying? That is exactly what I already had!

Even his son was afraid of him, his daughter in law certainly was, and no-one was immune from his intoxicated ranting. I came to hate going in to work, and when ultimately was allocated a company car so I could visit branches and make funeral arrangements in people's homes would grip the steering wheel so tightly that my knuckles would go white. The frustration at my predicament even manifested itself into a stammer, something it took me a long time to lose even after this foul family had left my sphere.

The company was a member of the Croydon District of the National Association of funeral directors, a very active area with quarterly meetings that were very well attended. Fortunately by the time I arrived at the firm the father regarded himself above such meetings, leaving them to his son. These were always subsidised by the petty cash, which was their own way of meeting any and all personal expenses. This included the weekly Tuesday 9.30am hairdresser appointment for the son's wife, a complete waste of money bearing in mind her otherwise disregard for her personal appearance.

It was a strange atmosphere in the office, different levels of importance. There were the main board directors from South London head office, who were treated with respect on their occasional visits. There was the father, with his one share in the business. There was the son and his wife. And then there was Martin, Tina, and me. We were the worker drones, grateful for a job, appreciating everything that was done for us.

My role was a straightforward one, and Martin and I soon slipped into a kind of routine. With the six branches, we tended to conduct most of the funerals arranged by them, Martin living above one of the branches so responsible for these. On reflection, it was a very good grounding, we all certainly discovered the locations of all the remote churchyards, as well as taking all the funerals arranged out of the Croydon head office. The son and his wife would arrange these when they had to, but he didn't bother getting out that much, despite his title of area manager.

As part of my employment it was agreed that I would sit for my professional exams, which I passed first time in 1981, co-incidentally at the same sitting as Stuart, the Truelove garage mechanic. That was how I came to meet Mr. Tom, or known to the public as Thomas Hands Ebbutt, who wrote the original manual in the 1950s. He gave me a couple of sessions of tuition, but it was mainly due to the assistance of my wife Pam that I passed, as she would ask me more and more difficult questions about scenarios that would probably never occur. The manual and exam were more about legalities, a complete change to the current one where a lot of emphasis is on course and practical work.

***

One incident from my early days of employment with this firm still stands in my memory even now, vivid in its detail. I had to attend a house in Caterham on the Hill in the Surrey countryside to arrange the funeral of a 14 year old young lady. Her father was a very strong willed character, with health problems, taking many bright coloured tablets daily for his heart condition. The girl's name was Pauline, and I can also recall her surname, but nothing will be gained by mentioned that in this book. She had been looking for some sweets, and thinking that father's heart tablets were Smarties, had swallowed a mouthful. She died.

I had to go round to the house to arrange her funeral, and was somewhat surprised to enter the living room to see that a video was playing a movie. They didn't turn it off throughout me making the funeral arrangements. Bizarre. They sat me down in front of the t.v. so I had my back to it as the movie played, they turned the sound down to about half volume, so I had to speak a little louder to gain their attention. That was because their eyes were drawn to the movie, and I frequently had to repeat my questions because they hadn't paid sufficient attention.

I was there for about an hour and a half, fighting against the video. But I knew exactly what the film was. It was Warren Beatty and Julie Christie in 'Heaven Can Wait'.

The funeral service was held at the local Catholic Church, and most unusually for those days the priest had agreed to allow the whole proceedings to be recorded. This was so the tape could be sent to their home country of Nigeria and be seen by family back home. This was done by a local photographic company who had their own movie cameras, an innovative firm, and the whole funeral cost would have been considerable. The burial was in the local cemetery in a new grave, with over two hours of filming.

We had to attend many country churchyards, in many climatic conditions, so the excellent training manifested itself one December day. It was a poorly attended church service right out in the back of nowhere, with just the vicar, four family members, the hearse driver, and me. This really placed my initiative under great strain, because even though it was an average sized coffin, it was snowing. Not just snowing, but coming down in buckets, blanketing everywhere, making roads almost impossible to negotiate, and the car with the other three bearers breaking down. The hearse driver and I were on our own.

This meant that we had to negotiate the path from lych gate to altar with just the two of us. I had a chat with the vicar, the hearse driver, and the family. I explained the difficulty and strain we would be under, but with their cooperation we would be able to successfully proceed. If the coffin isn't too heavy, it is possible for two experienced men to carry it, one on the back right, the other on the front left. The weight distribution is even, it is just difficult to get it initially onto your shoulders. Once you start walking, it's fine, until you come to place it down. That is where the cooperation of the clergyman came in. The two trestles were placed at the head of the altar, and when we entered he took the rear one away so we could walk straight in. Covered in snow. When we removed the coffin from our shoulders, he put the trestle under, so the weight was now even on the two trestles.

After the service was over, the process was reversed. It was all completed in a very professional way, the family were satisfied, and we breathed a sigh of relief.

***

A few months later, I was with the same hearse driver when taking the coffin to a funeral at Surrey and Sussex Crematorium, located at Crawley, quite close to Gatwick Airport.

This was the most bizarre in all my forty years in the funeral profession.

The deceased was a man in his 50s who had died suddenly. The office that had arranged was close to the Sussex border with Surrey, and a half hour journey from branch to crematorium along pleasant leafy country lanes.

It was just the hearse driver and myself, with the coffin and flowers in the back. Pleasant day for a drive, what could possibly go wrong?

We had been going for about ten minutes when I was aware of a knocking from behind me. I looked at Tony the hearse driver and he looked at me. It definitely wasn't him. His hands were on the steering wheel, his legs and feet were clearly visible. No attempt at a gag at my expense, this was genuinely something strange occurring. I consulted the paperwork. The body had definitely been embalmed. The entry was ticked by the embalmer, no doubt there then. Tony shrugged his shoulders, as if to say 'no idea mate.' I shrugged my shoulders back as if to say 'me neither'.

We listened for another five minutes, the knocking was not as frequent, but we still couldn't trace its source. Nothing for it, I climbed into the back as the hearse was driving along. I listened, but there was nowhere it could possibly be coming from. Apart from inside the coffin. But that was impossible, of course. Wasn't it?

Feeling a right fool, I knocked on the side of the coffin. Nothing.

For the next five minutes, I knocked, but there was no other knocking in reply.

I sat back in my seat in the front, feeling a right idiot for knocking on the side of a coffin as the hearse was being driven along public roads, for all motorists and passers-by to witness. It must have been a bizarre and strange thing for people to see, but it had to be done.

Back in my seat, we looked at each other. A few more knocks. Then they stopped.

Go on, ask yourself, what would you have done? Would you have driven straight to the back of the crematorium chapel, opened the lid to check, while the mourners wanted to know what the hell was occurring? Of course you wouldn't. There was no way that I could source that knocking, it MIGHT have come from the coffin, but highly unlikely. Yes, the responsibility was mine, the decision was mine to make, and I decided that on the grounds of almost certainty and likelihood we drive up to the crematorium chapel as if nothing untoward had occurred, proceed with the funeral, while standing at the back of the chapel throughout the whole service listening for knocking from the front.

There was no further knocking, and to this day Tony and I have absolutely no idea what happened during that journey. I returned to the garage, speaking to the embalmer. He remembered the body, and was adamant that he had embalmed. My conscience is clear, but even now I just wonder what really went on.

***

Money was very tight, and it was just as well that I had a company car, a beige coloured two door Ford Escort. I used to chat to the owner of a local small business. Mick owned a shop that specialised in videos and c.b. radio. He was a very pleasant chap to talk to, quite small in stature but big on ideas. The shop was a small fronted one in a side street, and I would pop in for a chat and exchange of ideas. He was a few years younger than me, but had achieved quite a lot already. What I admired most was his ability to find pirated copies of new films, which he provided under the counter on a rental basis.

The c.b. radio business was what interested him, but didn't provide much of an income. But he was good at sourcing the latest movies, such as E.T., I seem to remember. The quality of the films was pretty good, and I was always hiring one for the night. Of course, this was completely illegal, but he had seen a market and acted on his instincts. Trading Standards would have had a field day if they had discovered, but they were after the bigger operators, also those who were actually pirating the movies and making the copies.

Mick had a bank of video machines in his back office so was always making second quality copies, still of a more than acceptable standard. One day Mick casually mentioned to me that he also had a round on a local Croydon council estate, where he would call on a Friday and hire out the movies. This was my opportunity for him to expand.

Some twelve months previously I had found a part time job on a Friday night where I called at people's houses and collected their weekly payment to a money lender. It was always pleasantly handled, never any suggestion of being heavy handed with errant customers. That just wasn't me, nor the business owner. He was a money lender with a shop that sold mainly electrical goods at vastly inflated prices on a weekly basis until it was cleared. The percentage rate was horrendous, but he had been in business for many years very successfully, knowing his customer base. They had to go into the shop to receive the cash or goods, I went round on a Friday to collect the weekly dues.

There were at least a dozen rounds, all the collectors were fit men with cars, so it was as well that I had my company vehicle. At the end of the round I was expected to either return to the shop that night, or early the next morning. It was all very civilised, but I had noticed that more and more of my customers had video machines.

Mick and I had a very amicable conversation, where it was agreed he would provide all the tapes, and I would provide the customers. I would visit them on a Friday night and Monday night, they would pay £1 per tape, unless it was stronger, then £2. There were a lot of customers for the hard core material. Mick and I would split 50/50, and this arrangement worked very well for a considerable time. However, I read papers, and the Croydon Advertiser ran a series of news articles concerning the activities and prosecutions by the Trading Standards Office. They had already rounded up the bigger operators, and were looking at the next level. Mick's level. He had seized the opportunity I had presented him with, and now had a dozen men like me going round the local council estates. The writing was on the wall, I could see the time was right to end this little business opportunity. I handed all the tapes back to Mick, we shook hands and parted very amicably.

He had a very long think, and decided that maybe I was right, so he sold his empire to a competitor, along with the video rounds, the machines, the customers. It didn't bother me, he was welcome to do what he wanted, so I was particularly pleased to read about three months later that Trading Standards had raided a premises belonging to the foreign man who had bought Mick out. We had both exited well.

***

You always hurt the one you love, the one you shouldn't hurt at all, you always take the sweetest rose and crush it till the petals fall, you always break the kindest heart with a hasty word you can't recall, so if I broke your heart last night, it's because I love you most of all.

These are the words to the 1957 hit from the Mills Brothers, and then Clarence 'Frogman' Henry, and were the background to the most poignant funeral I ever attended.

It was 1982, with the venue the South London Crematorium. I had arranged the funeral at my office, so knew the background to the family tragedy. The deceased was a man in his early 40s, and he had decided to commit suicide. The method is unimportant, the relevant fact is that he was successful, so I had arranged his funeral with his two daughters and one son.

Until a few months previously it had been a very happy, secure family unit, but then he had discovered his wife's infidelity. She had been thrown out of the marital home not just by her husband, but also by the three children, who were devastated by their mother's adultery. The son was by this time married, but the two daughters were still living at home, very protective of their abandoned father. They blamed their mother for everything, dad's deterioration both mentally and physically, his devastation at suddenly becoming alone after many years of supposed happy marriage.

Dad just couldn't cope without his wife, tried reconciliation, but she was very happy in her relationship with a younger man who paid her more physical attention than her boring husband.

This all came out when I was making the funeral arrangements with the three children, because dad decided to end it all, unable to cope on his own.

He had left behind strict instructions for his wife to be denied funeral access, as he blamed her for everything, a sentiment shared of course by the siblings, so this was a funeral I conducted with some trepidation. Like everyone else, I hope that she would not attend and do the decent thing.

The funeral service was conducted by a clergyman sympathetic to the family, ignoring the circumstances as some strict men of the cloth at this time refused to take the service of someone who took their own life, though this viewpoint was increasingly become rarer.

We arrived at the crematorium chapel with ten minutes to spare, and there was no-one meeting the ex-wife's description. I can't refer to her as the widow in the circumstances, even though to be strict she was. The coffin was carried in, mourners followed, music played, we exited, the service commenced. We waited outside the chapel door, and one minute after the service started the lady arrived. Alone. I was in something of a dilemma, because a funeral crematorium chapel is a public place, and as such it is difficult to bar entrance to any member of the public, whatever circumstances might be prevalent. There is no way that you can stop someone attending a funeral service unless you employ bouncers to physically bar them, and then point of law is moot. My instructions had been very clear from the family however, but I had told them that despite my desire to comply with their wishes, neither me or my staff would place ourselves in a position to physically stand in the way should their mother wish to attend.

I opened the door for her.

She sat quietly at the back, making no sound, no-one was aware that she was there, until they saw the vicar's eyes move to the back row, which was their cue to all turn their heads round and stare. She averted her eyes, refusing to make any form of contact.

The whole service occurred with her sitting alone in the back row. The proceedings ended, I opened the door, the clergyman led everyone out, but to my amazement she continued sitting there, as they all filed past. No-one spoke to her, no-one looked at her, she just might as well have not been there. But they all knew the poignancy. Because of the music.

The three children had chosen this specifically. Playing loudly as they exited the crematorium chapel the Mills Brothers were singing the words at the beginning of this section. Read them again. Go onto YouTube and listen. I defy you not to be moved. This was the most touching funeral I have ever been involved with.

***

I have no idea what the regulations are now, but in the period covered, the Institute for Anatomical Research was governed by various restrictions concerning the disposal of remains donated to them. The situation was quite simple. People would donate their bodies for research purposes, with the best of intentions, but due to the volume, they had to be selective. More elderly people would wish this course of action, but there is only so much you can learn from the causes of death of old age, they preferred to have those who had been younger, so a lot of the time they politely declined. However, the terms of receiving a body under these circumstances dictated that they had to have a funeral of the remains that existed within two years, and bear all costs.

There was a contract for this funeral service, with my parent company in Clapham having it. This meant that every few days a plain white van would turn up at South London crematorium with four or six coffins. Families were given the option of attending, but they never did, and the duty clergyman at the crematorium was given the task of saying the final farewell, even if there was no-one in attendance. That was the contract.

The first service would be at 8am, with the van doors opened, three men carrying the coffin into the chapel, behind the clergyman. There were two of these connected to the crematorium, one was an elderly retired gentleman, very small in stature, very mean in disposition. His vestments were rarely clean, his hair shoulder length, straggly, dirty, his shave occurred later on in the day and I suspect his cleanliness habits occurred at the same time, because he growled at having to be there at such an unpleasant hour. He would drag his feet slowly, so those unfortunate to be carrying a heavy coffin had the weight on their shoulders for a greater length of time.

The time of his service would be five minutes maximum, which would contain the committal words. He would bow in a perfunctory way as he left the chapel, ready for the next one. That occurred ten minutes later. As well as his main south London retirement home, he had a cottage somewhere in the Dorset countryside which he would scuttle down to as frequently as he possibly could.

The other rota clergyman was a very dapper man. Tall, distinguished, about twenty years the junior of the other, his perfectly cut hair was always in place despite wind rain and an early hour. His clothing was always immaculate, and he was prepared on every morning for the possibility that families might attend. He did not want to be taken by surprise, so as well as the standard five minute funeral service he conducted every time, he also had the notes to hand of every arrangement, even if he didn't require this prop.

Befitting his wealth, as well as the more than adequate local house, he had an apartment in Spain, and you would always know when it was his turn because you would hear his perfectly preserved E-Type Jaguar driving up, parking in the car park away from the leaves and sticky gum, and when he had earned his fee for his six funerals in an hour would roar away in a cloud of loud vintage exhaust smoke.

However, because of his manners and demeanour he gained far more respect from the funeral and crematorium staff, but for one failing, shared by both men.

Every week, they would pore over the numbers of contracted funerals occurring at the South London crematorium, and if one had officiated at even more than one more than the other, then each would complain loudly and long, so the balance was restored the next month.

No public were ever aware of this daily private performance, because it happened in front of an audience of funeral and crematorium staff before anyone turned up.

***

When you are a funeral director, you have to be very adaptable. This stood me in very good stead when I was seconded to the head offices in South London for a few days. They were short of senior conducting staff, and I willingly went there to assist. Most of the funerals I conducted went without a hitch, nothing in my memory at all, until I took a service conducted by Bishop Timothy.

He was a larger than life character, it was a simple life if you just let him get on with it.

Bishop Timothy was a Ghanaian gentleman, I suspect that he was never actually ordained, and that his title was a self-appointed one. His strength was in his personality and being a very strong orator. His Sunday services were always standing room only, his flock were completely devoted to him, so if he wasn't actually a Bishop, then who cared? The firm certainly took him seriously, giving him whatever he wanted, something I was to experience.

One of his parishioners had died, no memory about them, but the funeral stands out for me. I was with the hearse driver, who had fitted it out according to instructions and previous funerals organised by Bishop Timothy. We reported to the house, where the body had been reposing for the previous 24 hours, so he organised his male flock to carry it to the hearse waiting outside the front door. No cars, we walked all the way from the house to his church, which was about two miles away. No sense of time or distance, they didn't matter, what was more relevant was the chanting and the procession. Because the back door of the hearse was open, and connected to the cigarette lighter power supply was a cassette, playing chanting hymns at full blast. The back door was open because there were two ghetto blaster speakers alongside the coffin in the back.

I was allowed to walk alongside Bishop Timothy in front of the hearse, the leading lady members of his choir were right behind, belting out all their favourites. They knew all the words, it took what seemed to be an interminable time before we were at the front steps of his church. I just let them get on with it, they carried the coffin into the church without any supervision, which would have been pointless in any case. When it had started, with the church doors wide open so those outside could listen in, I sat in the front seat of the hearse with the driver and ate my lunch.

The men of the congregation had been consuming large amounts of alcohol during the morning, so there was a steady stream of them coming out of the church. The fact that there was no lavatory wasn't a problem, because there was an outer church wall, very convenient and utilised for the next couple of hours. Never seen this before or since.

The hearse driver and I nudged each other, 'Here they come then', the coffin was unsteadily conveyed to the back door of the hearse, dumped inside with a loud whack, and that was it. No more music, a more sedate drive to the crematorium, with a lot more service for the next allotted half hour. Then we were allowed to go.

This was my only experience of the famous Bishop Timothy. I have tried to research him as part of this story, but he seems to have disappeared into legend.

***

I have said that there were no other memorable instances during my week at head office, but after writing the above have remembered another incident, bizarre, but true. Clapham is a very diverse area, with many residents from a variety of backgrounds. I conducted this particular funeral for a Greek family.

There was nothing particularly notable about them, apart from their volatility, not the men, but the women, and there had been a family feud going on for years. Four of the women just could not stand each other, their men did as they were told, so back up their wives as well. I was completely unaware of this background and history, until we arrived at the cemetery.

The main part of the funeral had been a full requiem Catholic mass, lasting almost two hours. A normal Mass will be just under an hour, but those involving the full Mass for those of stronger faith and committal to the church would last twice as long, with a larger number of priests to officiate. Of course, they were aware of the background, but didn't bother to inform me, so I was completely taken aback by what occurred.

As you will probably know already, inside a Catholic church there is a certain hierarchy, with senior priests taking the more prominent role, leaving the menial tasks to the junior men. As they knew there was a strong possibility of unpleasantness, the prayers at the graveside were delegated to a more lowly priest, so it wouldn't matter if he had to contend with a problematic situation.

The interment and committal part of the proceedings were over, all that was left was for the gravediggers to fill in the grave before we left. This was becomingly increasingly rare, but for those who wanted, then it was not discouraged. But the four warring women didn't like the way that the gravediggers were shovelling the earth in. They thought that there was insufficient care and attention, so one of the younger ones snatched the spade, hitched up her black skirt, threw her black hat at her husband, and proceeded to ruin her shoes with mud as she placed the earth into the deep grave.

Not to be outdone, another woman did the same. Then a third. There were only three shovels, so the fourth lady didn't hesitate, she snatched the spade from the first woman, the one who had started it all. Now there were three weapons. Number two aimed hers with a back movement against number three, my, that blow must have hurt her. Number four then hit number two. Spadeless number one was behind number three, who was standing alongside the grave. Number one shoved number three in the back. She toppled in, on the way down being relieved of her shovel. Number one then shovelled earth into the grave on top of number three. By this stage there were three women, all dressed in black, all with lethal weapons, all attacking each other. Now, I ask you, what would you have done? Yup, I did exactly the same as the priest. Nothing. If they wanted to whack hell out of each other, let them get on with it. The men however did intervene, snatching the spades from the women. Another two men reached into the grave, helping out number three. They stood around, sheepish, not really knowing what to do next.

One of their men gave the spade to one of the open mouthed gravediggers, then the other two were returned, normal service was resumed, and pretty soon all went their separate ways. Nothing was said between me and the priest. Anything would have been superfluous.

***

In early 1983 there was an upheaval in the firm. A Yorkshire funeral director also owned a business that provided the firm with coffins, and he bought into the business as a major shareholder and director. My boss was all over him, private lunches, chats in the back office, and then one day my boss and his wife were gone. Just like that. They sold their home, taking their children and dogs with them to take over the position of area manager for his Yorkshire business.

I had seen my boss in operation, I knew what he was capable of, or should I say more like what his shortcomings were, and it was pretty obvious to anyone with half a brain that he had burnt his Surrey bridges, never to return. What a wonderful day for the firm, especially as there was now a vacancy as area manager. Yup, I got the job, and loved it.

The position involved answering to the main board, and it was a great time for me. The Yorkshire director was one of my bosses, and we struck up a particularly good accord. I had a lot of respect for him, despite his mental aberration by employing my previous boss and his wife, and it gave me a lot of pleasure when after about a year we heard that all was not well in the Yorkshire empire, due to liberties being taken. Initial boundaries had been set, but these had been breached, so a parting of the ways occurred.

I got on very well with Doug, the workshop and garage foreman. He had been with the firm for many years, through upheavals, change of company ownership, and every now and again he would tell me that the workshop had some broken coffins, ostensibly delivered in this state and accepted in error, or more realistically damaged by his clumsy staff. One of these was a lovely fellow with the nickname the Milkman.

That had been his previous occupation, but he couldn't take the early mornings. Funeral life suited him better, but he was very short-sighted with milk bottle glasses, also very short in stature. I liked him, perhaps I usually try to protect the underdog, as he was particularly picked on by the unpleasant patriarch with one share, who was the archetypical bully, picking on those who couldn't respond. The Milkman by this stage was a lot freer of this nastiness, because once his son had decamped to Yorkshire, his influence in the company waned. I actively discouraged the bully from coming to the office after his drunken lunches, usually with great success.

Doug the foreman had to somehow dispose of these coffins. They were only usually slightly damaged, perhaps with unsightly scratches, but they were always intact. There was a popular trait many years ago for coffins to be covered in a discreet coloured velvet, so when making arrangements with families, if they were of a certain age and background, I would offer them a velvet covered coffin at no extra charge. They were very satisfied, as they were getting something for nothing, Doug and me were very happy because we had managed to improve the funeral experience for families while depleting the workshop of stock that could not normally be used.

As area manager, the next year passed all too fast, but this was all to change when a London business asked me if I would like to go and work for them. It was the next step in my funeral career.

Traditions, Tales, and Strange Occurrences

There are many stories attached to funerals, old tales that have substance, some with none at all. The first I mention here concerns flowers, and I will continue to give more contemporary examples.

The early Victorians had a fear of being buried alive. How true I have no idea, but there were some reported instances of exhumations occurring and heavy scratch marks on the top of the inside of the coffin lid. Unpopular cremations didn't start until the late 1870s, so it was exclusively interments. Chapels of rest became increasingly popular, with a piece of string attached to the hand of the deceased, the unsealed lid slightly askew, and the other end of the string attached to a loud bell, so if the hand moved so the bell would ring.

There would be many coffins in the large chapel, perhaps as many as fifty in densely populated areas, with the coffins lying for up to a week. The lowly paid attendants were there purely for one reason – to listen out for a bell ringing. This could be disconcerting, because it is not that well known that bodies can move with the fluids settling, so the attendant would likely get bored pretty quickly and not bother to look too closely, thereby defeating the object of the exercise. What made the situation more unpleasant was the fact that embalming was expensive and unpopular, so after a week the large chapel with vast numbers of cadavers became extremely unpleasant to enter.

The Victorian solution was simple and largely effective. Have flowers in the chapel to hide the malodorous odours.

The flowers were the property of each family of course, with no-one wanting to donate for the good of all, so when the coffin was removed for interment, the flowers went with it. Human nature being what it is, each family would like to out-do the other, spending more money on elaborate coffins, with glass sided hearses so everyone could see that a lot of money had been spent. It wasn't too long before flowers entered the situation.

With a large chapel with many coffins on show, Victorians wanted to make their floral tributes more elaborate as well. The larger the better, because they had spent more than anyone else, because they had loved the deceased more than the other families. As the tributes became more expensive, there was more thought into the design. The name of the deceased in large letters was very common, and one of the most popular floral tribute designs was the Pearly Gates. This was a minimum of two feet high, and could easily be five feet. There would be green moss covering a firm wire base, with the main structure being two framed gates, not locked, slightly open to symbolise that the deceased had already entered. There would be white lilies decorating the gates, with a dove on each of the two gate posts. Arum lilies became associated with funerals because of this design.

The Pearly Gates tribute remains popular in the 21st Century, albeit in a simpler form. The doves are still there, the gates are thin strips of metal, the moss base is moist to keep the whole arrangement as fresh for as long as possible, but the size is smaller, with anything over two feet tall somewhat rare. Ostentation is not the order of the day any more.

Floral tributes in the early part of the 21st Century are mainly confined to those placed for show on the coffin so it is not stark and bare. Those attending in the main donate to a charity of the family's choice in the form of a cheque to the funeral director, who collates, sends to the charity, who then acknowledge to the family with a list of donations.

For many years it was the custom to ask the funeral director to arrange for floral tributes to be delivered to hospital or nursing home, but as transport costs mounted this service was no longer free. Once families realised that they were going to have to pay for this additional service they decided it was no longer necessary, so they are usually left to die and then disposed of by the crematorium staff. Charities don't mention this additional donation when acknowledging their increasing income. Funny that.

***

One of the most common questions I have been asked over the past forty years is 'what happens to the coffin and body? Are they burned? Whose ashes do I get back? Let's give one long answer.

Over the past forty years, cremators have become far more compatible with the environment. The tall chimneys would belch out black or gray smoke, and there was a pervasive smell only associated with crematoria. It is something that I have not smelled for many years, and if I did then I would immediately connect with attending funerals in the 1970s and 1980s. The ash would hang in the air, and if you stayed around long enough you would find it in your clothing, as well as your hair. It was not particularly healthy for the people who worked there full time, with the class of employee being particularly low and common. They just could not get anyone else to work there with a healthy employment market outside the crematorium gates. However, they did very well for tips, because every single funeral handed over a £1 gratuity, so with for example South London Crematorium in London SW16 having three chapels, on a busy day there could be as much as £30 - £40 to be shared between the staff. The time allotted for each service was 30 minutes, and woe betide any undertaker who was late, or any clergyman who overstayed his time.

Even as long ago as covered here, the standards were mainly high. Every coffin was kept separate from the others, cremated individually, which on a busy day could mean that the staff had to stay until 8 or 9 in the evening to keep on top of their workload. Another reason why staff were difficult to come by.

At the end of the service the coffin would be rolled into a vacant cremator. The heat would already be intense, far too hot for humans to touch the inside, the door would be shut and sealed, the gas level increased so pretty soon the wood would burn to nothing. There would be an observation panel in the door, with the coffin contents gradually disintegrating off the rollers onto the bottom. Gas is turned off, ventilation opened to let heat and gases out, when sufficiently cool door is opened and contents removed from the base and placed in a secure receptacle. The remains are not a lot, when hot black, when cool a strange murky gray. Now they are at a manageable temperature, they are placed in a grinder, so the remains are more powdered, but still not as fine as ash, or sand. More like grit. That is what is returned to the family on request, or scattered on the rose garden of remembrance if instructed. It is far too hot to be returned the same day.

Diligence would make way for expediency and there was one particular crematorium I frequently visited that had a large bin in the back, where the ashes were topped up. When families wanted them returned for private disposal, a suitable amount were scooped and placed in a plastic urn. This was the only place where it was practiced, and by the early 1980s had been abandoned.

One lady who had lost her husband three months previously had a caller at her door. He was a military historian, and had purchased her late husband's medals at auction. He wanted to research further, so the auction house had provided him with her contact details. Bear in mind that this was the mid 1980s, freedom of information was a lot less stringent, so a request of this nature would usually be granted. She was aghast, because she had placed his medals on his suit in the funeral director's chapel of rest, prior to the coffin being sealed ready for cremation.

Both the medal collector and widow contacted the police, because he was unhappy at unwittingly being involved in a crime of this nature. It transpired that the cremator operator was in the custom of opening the coffin when no-one was around in the hope that there would be something of value inside. He discovered the medals, selling them at auction. Very easy to trace the crime, he was taken to court, and given a custodial sentence. The crematorium had to apologise profusely, were severely embarrassed, so had to change their flawed operating procedures. Lesson learned.

These are the only two instances in forty years of malpractice, both remedied.

***

We had a hearse driver who was a very solemn man. At this time he was in his early thirties, unmarried, taking his job very seriously. He was always smart, polished shoes to a shine that reflected the way that he conducted his job. I had my eye on him for promotion, as he was such a worthy candidate.

Bob had been working for the firm for a couple of years when we had a funeral to a main cemetery in Windsor in Berkshire. It was well over an hours' journey, so of course we allowed plenty of extra time for eventualities such as traffic or those difficult to predict. The journey went without a hitch, so we parked up by the roadside for half an hour or so. Five minutes before the appointed time, we were at the cemetery gates, rolling gently along the driveway to the chapel entrance. We had hired in three men from a local funeral company, this was a very common practice in the funeral profession as this method is far cheaper than transporting and paying wages for three of your own staff. Suitably dressed, the men were standing to one side, as the family and other mourners were waiting in the doorway with the clergyman who would be officiating. All passed in the professional, uneventful way.

The service itself was unmemorable, the local hired staff are just a passing impression from many years ago, I can remember the cemetery, as it was the only time in forty years that I visited it. I can also remember the graveside, because it was here that the memorable incident occurred.

The bearers carried the coffin from chapel to graveside without incident, it was placed on the ground, the webbing was threaded between the handles, and then gently swung over the open grave, ready to receive its gift for time immemorial. That is when something out of the ordinary occurred.

As Bob bent over the open grave, one part of the webbing in his hand, something fell out of the inside breast pocket of his jacket, despite the fact that it was buttoned. It happened so fast,

I looked at Bob, he looked at me, nothing more than a glance. I looked at the vicar, no reaction, mourners likewise, nothing for it, we just had to continue. There would have been too much disruption to proceedings in any case to pause for something so trivial. Sometimes you have to make instant decisions, and stand by them, That is what I did here, I did not pause or stop, all carried on in the usual way.

The gravedigger started filling in the grave with all still present, which were the instructions.

The hired in bearers went, so did the vicar, so did the mourners, it just left me and Bob sitting in the hearse as we were about to drive away. I couldn't resist asking

'what fell in the grave Bob?'

'a cassette tape from my inside pocket'.

'that was unlucky.' A pause. 'Who was the tape by?'

'My favourite group'

'and they are?'

'the Grateful Dead

***

What goes in the coffin stays in the coffin

The following part covers many years, and I am quite certain that others involved in the funeral profession over the years have many more incidents they can share.

I can remember one particular family that spoke very fondly of their relative in such a glowing way that they wanted something different placed in the coffin with him. Six bottles of brown ale. Unopened. It was to be a burial, so there was no problem, they provided us with the booze, we placed them in with him for his eternal journey. With an opener.

The system must work. Bear in mind that on average there are in the region of 610,000 funerals annually, with temptation and human nature going hand in hand, so it's a wonder to me that decency and morality prevail as they do in an ever increasing dissolute society.

Returning to humour, I heard of an incidence where the family brought the clothing into the office so it could be dressed on the deceased, and when the family came in to view, when they left the chapel of rest they turned to the arranger and said 'he looked really lovely, but why did he have a calculator in his hands?'

The reply was 'we assumed he was an accountant or bookkeeper, so ensured that it was placed between his hands as a lasting tribute.'

'no, he was a lorry driver.'

Upon investigation, it transpired that the clothing had been placed on an office desk, and when gathered the office calculator had been mistakenly picked up as well.

Pacemakers have been a problem since they were invented, especially the early ones. There was an incidence in the early days in the Midlands when the funeral company was not informed by the family that the deceased had been one of the pioneer recipients, so was not removed by the embalmer for some unexplained reason. I would have thought it was pretty obvious to the simplest brain that er, there's a pacemaker, perhaps I should remove it? But no, it remained, and went into the cremator. That gets pretty hot, 1000 degrees Centigrade, so the pacemaker went bang, disintegrated, creating a lot of damage to the internal workings.

What happens to any jewellery that has been left on the body? That has been cremated as well, whatever is in the coffin gets burned, and after a little while, say a few months, when the cremator is serviced, there might be a small gold deposit remaining. This is removed and sold for charitable purposes. But there is very little, because gold melts at this intensity of heat.

Here's a strange fact that not many people even in the funeral profession are aware of. Some families want the ashes returned so they may scatter themselves at some favourite location. Don't scatter close to dogs, as there is something in the ashes that is attractive to them, so they come calling and sniffing, which of course could prove to be potentially distressing.

The strangest disposal of the cremated remains occurred when I arranged the funeral of a middle aged wealthy gentleman who was very close to his wife – and his vintage MG pre WW2 sports car. It was red, garaged, and his pride and joy. She wanted the ashes returned so they could be sealed in the glove compartment. I did feel sufficiently emboldened to ask various questions such as what happens if the car is stolen, or what happens when you come to sell the car. Her replies were quite matter of fact and logical, along the lines of what will be will be.

It is just not possible for every family to have ashes scattered on the centre circle of a favourite football pitch. All requests are denied for obvious reasons. If you want to transport the ashes from one country to another, my advice is to ask for the certificate from the crematorium, and take them in your hand luggage. In today's heightened airline security situation, this might not be so practical, perhaps place them in your suitcase, so they go in the hold. You can also have them couriered by a reputable international company, but ensure that all relevant documentation for the country of destination is in order. Sometimes this also entails a visit to an embassy, with the extra fees.

The laws concerning scattering of remains at sea are not nearly so stringent as those relating to burial at sea of a coffin. If you have your own boat, you just anchor up, and scatter. If you have to hire a boat, then the same principal applies. I have also known cruise ship passengers wanting ashes to be scattered on a voyage. This is arranged very discreetly by the ship's personnel, and is usually conducted while the ship is in port, as while at sea there is the potential for distress to be caused. Suitable words are said by the appropriate officer, while a crew member conducts the scattering. It is quite normal for a gratuity to be given as a way of saying thank you for performing something above and beyond the usual call of duty.

***

Burial at sea, and scattering of ashes at sea

At the time of writing, there are only two places around the coast of the UK where burial at sea is permitted. One is off Newhaven, in East Sussex, not that far away from Brighton, and the other is close to The Needles, off the Isle of Wight. The reason for these two locations is that the tide is far less likely to return the coffin to shore. There is a third location off Northumberland, but that is only allowed when the two mentioned are not available.

I don't want to go into too much detail here, as it is not particularly relevant to this anecdotal story of mine, but I only ever buried one coffin at sea, many years ago, it was not particularly memorable, as all went off in a dignified uneventful way. I booked the Sussex boat, we arrived early, we had a clergyman aboard to say his words, the sea and tidal swell were very kind, all was completed as it should have been. Not too sure what would have happened if the occasion had been during the winter months, however, as I am quite sure that the boat doesn't go out if the forecast is for bad weather.

KAT

The initials stand for Kenyon Air Transportation. The office was in Chiltern Street, parallel to Baker Street. The office is opposite the building that used to be the Chilton Street Fire Station, which closed down some years now and is one of the trendiest most expensive London restaurants.

I have not been back for over 25 years, but in my day it was a double shop front, all on the ground floor, with a basement. This was the casket showroom, the stairs were too narrow, so fortunately there was a pavement cellar door, which was swung open to reveal the showroom below. We would slide the casket down, place it on the trestles, which would be covered. The wealthier clients would be taken down the internal stairs, select the casket, and when it was ready to be received at head office workshops all hands would be available to manhandle it up the ramp again to the waiting hearse parked half on double yellow lines, half on the pavement.

The right side of the office was for staff and their desks, the back area was the office of the manager, with the left side of the building the arranging area and our staff refreshment area behind.

I got the job because I was head hunted. J.H. Kenyon was the parent company, and the principals were gentlemen businessmen. They had been funeral directors for many generations, with great influence in the London business community. To mark this respect, many years previously they had been appointed as official funeral directors to the Royal Family. If you ever asked yourself if the Royal Family have their own hearses, staff, equipment and premises on permanent stand-by, the answer is no. They have a contract with a respected company with traditions of discretion, which is now with another London firm. In my time, the chairman would be summoned to the Lord Chamberlain's office for the account to be disseminated, scrutinised in such great detail that this could easily take a morning. On one occasion he discreetly asked if the company might be granted a Royal Warrant, as they were the only firm that were exclusively used. The answer was that this might be considered an unwise move, as any advertising, discreet or otherwise, was frowned upon.

Kenyons were instructed for the arrangements of Royal servants as well, with the Palace picking up the bill. These people usually lived in grace and favour apartments connected with palaces such as Kensington and Hampton Court, had retired but continued in Royal service if they possibly could for as long as they could. Service was in their blood, and as a mark of this the reward was to be looked after right to very end. They knew that they would be looked after by Kenyons.

Michael Kenyon was the chairman, his cousin (I think) Christopher was a director and head of KAT, and there was another Kenyon who with his wife were branch managers in Westbourne Grove. Michael's son Peter was younger, recently arrived in the firm, and destined for greater responsibility.

If you worked for J.H. Kenyon, you were considered to be at the top of your profession, you could not possibly improve elsewhere. Even better still was to work at Kenyon Air Transportation, because this office was for the best.

Kenyon Air Transportation had been founded in the 1930s to meet a need. Air travel was expanding, and the crashes were increasing. As funeral directors to the Royal Family, the company were in an ideal position to appreciate that a firm with connections was required to assist authorities when a disaster occurred. This widened over the years until my arrival in August 1984. By that time KAT was mainly used for repatriations to and from all over the world. If a foreign national died in London, then KAT would inevitably be involved. If a British national died anywhere in the world then it was highly likely that KAT would be involved not just in repatriating them back to the UK, but actively involved in either local funeral arrangements, or acting under instruction from a local funeral company.

I won't try to fog the issue here, but start with an example from my very first day, August 4th 1984.

My immediate boss was Phil, who had been with KAT for many years. We were the same age, and I immediately liked him. He was tall, thin, and full of nervous energy. The office was only a small one, with a shop entrance from the street. There was a private office at the very back of the room, occupied by Mike R., who had interviewed me. He was a little older, and Phil's desk was right outside his door. Mike's knowledge was not as great as Phil's, and he relied on him for a lot. He was more of a gentleman, but this was not the same kind of set-up as my previous office. These people were gentlemen with manners and intelligence.

I was sent to an apartment overlooking Hampstead Heath to receive payment on an account that was £4,982. I remember the amount very well.

The bus went quite close to the address, and then there was a last mile walk across the Heath. There was a grass pathway alongside the very busy road, and the address was a stand-alone building with superb panoramic views. As it was summer, there had been little recent rain, so no mud underfoot. I was wearing a suit, with tie, clean polished shoes, very respectable and professional. There was a very wide front door, which opened to my approach, and I was greeted by a very tall African gentleman who was very well dressed, with suit, tie, and also polished shoes. He had a colleague not so well presented, who was obviously muscle without the intelligence and authority.

They asked my business, and then proceeded to frisk me for anything dangerous that may be used against their employer. The reason for the repatriation back to Nigeria had been assassination, so no-one was taking any chances any more. The underling stood to one side as I was escorted into the lift that was hidden in the corner of the huge waiting area, otherwise full of furniture and a desk in the doorway. The lift had no buttons, being controlled by an as yet unseen person in an upper floor. The door opened, to reveal this man standing there, again in suit, tie, and polished shoes. A uniform, then.

I was led to a very tall, distinguished looking gentleman who was obviously the man in charge. He shook my hand, and asked me for the account, which I duly presented. He then said

'Would you like a drink?'

Bear in mind that this was 10am on my first day, and I had no idea what to expect.

My reply was a very politely said 'no thank you sir'.

He forcefully said 'You will have a drink'.

'Thank you sir, a gin and tonic if I may.'

He looked at one of his people, who immediately came forward with a tray, on it an unopened bottle of Booths gin, another unopened bottle of tonic, a glass that looked and felt as if it came from a set provided by Waterford, and a dish of ice. He nodded at me, and then disappeared, giving me the opportunity of looking properly at my surroundings. I was in a huge room, probably forty feet across, with the whole of the front wall a glass panoramic view. The vista was of Hampstead Heath, and you could literally see for miles. This place was worth a fortune.

The room was split into four levels. I was at the back of the room, looking down into the lounge area, with lots of leather sofas, arm chairs, wooden floor covered by rugs. Nothing matched, it was just a hotch potch that looked as if it had been designed by someone with even less colour sense than me. The upper level by the window had some more seating, this time a dining room table that could seat at least a dozen, then further round to the left another smaller dining room table for only six. There were also some leather chairs facing out onto the Heath.

The kitchen level was out of my peripheral vision, but I was aware it was over to the right somewhere at the back of the room, on another level. The client had disappeared into one of the bedrooms, which was on a middle fourth level, with views I assumed of the front of the property, also with more stunning vistas. I hadn't been appreciating the view for more than five minutes when he returned, this time with two sealed Nat West plastic bank enveloped with £2,500 each in cash. That made £18 in change to be handed over. I didn't have it.

I patted my pockets, and apologetically thanked him for the payment. He made a dismissive gesture with his right hand as he waved away the attempt at apology for the lack of change. So I had a tip of £18 just for collecting an account. I thanked him, and was just about to leave when he stopped me. He said

'You've forgotten something.'

Bemused, I replied 'I don't think so, sir.'

He gestured at the gin bottle.

'Take it with you.'

***

This was to be my introduction to another world, where largesse and gratuities were commonplace. The opulence and luxury were extreme, one inhabited by few English. A typical day would involve arranging repatriations to any country in the world, or maybe taking a London funeral, or maybe being instructed by an Embassy or local private hospital such as The Harley Street Clinic.

There was a saloon car as a company office runabout, which was used to take clients from hospital to registrar's office to embassies to airports, anywhere necessitating the smooth passage of documentation. It was fortunate that I had already quite a good working knowledge of London, which was to be extended greatly during my period of employment with the company. Summer could be the busiest time for repatriations, because in early Spring the Arab households would decamp to London before it got too hot in their home countries. They would also require private treatments, often liver related involving excess consumption of alcohol, the operations sometimes failing which was where my office became involved. My view on life became sceptical, realising that clients from a non-English background would fudge the truth in any way so they gain their successful wishes. An excellent example of this involved a family from Bahrain.

There were two brothers connected to the Embassy, and their mother had come to London for an operation. This was not a success, and the two brothers were on the diplomatic list. That was for the privileged few, doors opened for them, formalities bypassed, troublesome documentation ignored, so as their mother had suddenly died they wanted her to be added to the diplomatic list. Posthumously. They did everything they possibly could to have her added retrospectively, but the Foreign Office would have none of it. Diplomatic representation was made in a very senior way, to no avail. It had never been done before, and no precedent was going to be created for anyone. No matter their background, country, or influence. It just wasn't going to happen, and I saw all this evolve because I was sitting in their Knightsbridge apartment, waiting.

Part of my job was to wait patiently while clients made up their minds what they were going to do. On this occasion, I was waiting patiently for the decision from the Foreign Office. So when the inevitable decision was made, I then had to escort them to the hospital to collect and complete the paperwork, then to the office of Registrar for Deaths then to the Embassy. This was a straightforward procedure, one I had conducted many times previously, but this arrangement stood out because of the transport arrangements being discussed.

As well as the Foreign Office negotiations, they were attempting to hire a plane for the journey back to Bahrain. I frequently had to escort the coffin and family from their London apartments to usually Heathrow airport, as they would close their London house to return home for the funeral, only leaving a small staff to maintain the home. What made this different was the difficulty they were experiencing in finding a plane to hire. There is a specialist brokering company, who after initially failing to find a London based plane extended their enquiries further into Europe. This again resulted in failure, a word the Bahrain family didn't understand. If they wanted something, they got it, and they were pretty miffed at the diplomatic list refusal. They just would not be denied, so in the end instead of hiring a plane, they bought one. For $11million. From Paris.

As soon as I had the green light when they accepted the diplomatic situation, I rushed round gaining the documentation, then the same day we were off to Heathrow. Maybe it is still there, but in those days, the mid 1980s, there was an area between terminals one and two for private jets and planes, with its own private waiting area. This is for the seriously rich, and I was a frequent visitor. The newly acquired Swissair 300 seater plane landed, and I escorted my hearse and driver to the bottom of the ramp. The family had no regard for the future sale of the plane, or its condition, so the next instruction was for the chief baggage handler to remove a row of seats at the back. These were discarded, never to be seen or used again on that plane, so then the coffin took its place, strapped securely to the floor. Once this was completed, the hearse driver and myself left the plane, the family boarding. We were not allowed to leave until the doors had been closed, and the head of the household had presented us with our obligatory gratuity. This took the form of two £50 notes. We were then allowed to leave, starving hungry, because I had not been in a refreshment situation all day, just managing to find the occasional toilet. It was gone nine, and I finally arrived home about eleven, after a fifteen hour stressful day.

***

The main front men were Phil in the office and Eddie who was the document driver. They had both worked for the firm for many years, were still aged about forty, approximately my age, but like me despite an excellent education were not gentlemen from the top drawer of society, not necessarily precluding promotion to main board director but without substantial financial funds it was unlikely that we were ever going to progress to the top slot. When we arranged repatriations to and from the UK every day, it could be for anyone with the ability to pay the fees. They may come from any echelon of life, and these memorable comparisons come from the same cemetery. St. Mary's next to West London crematorium.

This is a cemetery for people of the Catholic faith, and example number one concerns a family of travellers. As already mentioned, with forty years of funeral experience, I have only ever encountered an occasion where a gypsy caravan has been burned after the ceremonies. That was in Coulsdon in Surrey in 1978, when the head of the family passed away. The family I am writing about now were more from the Irish tinkers community.

There had been a feud between them and another family for many years, with violence only allowed after all formalities had been completed. The bereaved family and the other were to attend the funeral, because they had been traditionally close for many years, both based in West London, only uniting at weddings and funerals.

There was a strict protocol to be complied with, the agenda starting with each family taking over a local pub for three or four days while the arrangements were finalised. The landlord would have some heritage with each family, the till takings would be immense, with blonde-dyed haired women vying with their men to consume the greatest quantities of alcohol. The children ran everywhere unrestricted, arguments were allowed, but no physical contact. Knives and guns were allowed to be shown, but not used. Yet.

The pub would open by 8am, with breakfasts served. The car park would be taken over by that family and their vehicles, with an unspoken rule that outsiders were not allowed to be served. If you were a regular in that pub, tough, find somewhere else to drink for the next few days. All day into the late hours any licensing rules were conveniently suspended, no police attended to administer any infringements. There weren't sufficient suicidal police for this role. However, discreet police observation was maintained at each pub, so they were aware of numbers in anticipation of the subsequent outbreak of hostilities. Or should I say war.

There is a reasonable sized chapel in the cemetery for the service, overflowing on this occasion. I was the conductor, the man in charge, supervising. This was well within my capabilities and experience fortunately, as the occasion was so sensitive that one word could result in premature carnage despite the cease-fire. The secret of any successful funeral is always to ascertain the head person, man or woman, ask them the questions, so smooth procedures and continuity are maintained. That was the way here. The head man was the son of the deceased, the oldest brother of four, with a further three sisters. All with partners.

The men wore black suits, white shirts, narrow black ties askew with the shirt top button undone, polished black shoes. The women wore black skirts, patent leather shoes, white blouses, black jackets, dyed blonde hair. Both sexes had body piercings. Children were smartly dressed.

It was a warm spring day, no rain, starting at the pub with a horse drawn hearse followed by a flat bed lorry. Floral tributes organised for travellers funerals were the most ornate of the lot. Great prestige was attached to the complexity of design, I have seen many huge floral dart boards that were so heavy they would take two or sometimes three men to carry safely. This funeral even had the design of a horse and cart, the black flowers depicting the horse, real leather reins and saddle, the wooden cart covered in flowers. The wooden base was obviously very strong, and I insisted that some of the mourners carry it from the pub where we started to the flat bed lorry, where it stayed until after completion of ceremonies at the cemetery. Then it didn't matter. The more you read, the more you appreciate the complexity of successful funeral arrangements.

The procession from the pub to the cemetery was a long one. They were only a mile apart, but I had allowed for an hour. The mourners had already consumed copious amounts of alcohol by the 10am departure, so when we arrived at the cemetery gates there were a lot of derogatory comments when they saw a large police presence outside. This comprised four full minibuses, one coach, and the only time I ever saw a police helicopter hover over a funeral. That's right, they were filming everything from the air. They knew it was all going to kick off afterwards between the two pubs, and wanted to be ready.

The whole funeral went off without a hitch. We came away from the cemetery chapel, the priest kept them all well behaved, we walked to the grave, interment happened. Bizarre, with the police helicopter intrusively observing, and what was even more weird was the fact that there was an allotment overlooking the grave, with even more police watching. Nothing the mourners could do, apart from look daggers. Bad form to shout and gesticulate.

A very large cash tip of £250 was handed over to me, that would definitely not have occurred had they been dissatisfied. We all went back to the pub, we dropped them off, in anticipation of what was to come. That was where the police came in.

Darkness fell, they left their two pub strongholds, and armed with guns, knives, chains, bottles, hostilities commenced on a waste ground. The police knew it was going to occur, there was nothing they could do to stop, so they just let them get on with it. No-one was killed, quite a few broken bones, a lot of blood, casualty department was busy that night but they knew beforehand.

However, another day, another funeral, same cemetery, something completely different.

The famous entertainer Danny La Rue had a West End apartment in the middle of theatre land. His close friend and manager sadly passed away while in Australia, with KAT arranging for him to be brought back for funeral. One of the reasons I was invited to work in the office was my background as a funeral conductor, and it was usually me who took all the services from this office, wherever it might be in the UK. We arranged for the repatriation, with the funeral at the same West London cemetery. Fortunately again the weather was a superb day, with a very high attendance of every gay from the entertainment profession. It was an occasion to be seen, with plenty of mwah mwah on the cheeks as 'hello dahling' was sincerely uttered loudly. Most were in strong floral and colourful outfits, with my heterosexual staff maintaining professional straight faces.

No police helicopter, no minibuses full of butch coppers, just all the gay community from London's entertainment world gathered in one place. I can't list them all, there were too many, but I do remember Barry Howard from Hi de Hi and John Inman from Are You Being Served prominent in their presence. There was genuine love and affection for family and friends, so it was as well that plenty of time had been allowed for formalities. I remember that two limousines had been booked, so it was back to the theatreland apartment where we dropped them off.

Such a contrast, which made the office a very interesting and different one to work from.

***

Van Gogh painted eight different versions of Sunflowers, and I read an article about them in a newspaper some time ago whereby seven are either in museums, or private collections, with the whereabouts of one unknown. Despite the art world being fascinated by the location, I am one of the few people who have seen this missing Sunflowers, which came about in a mundane way taking me completely by surprise.

Work in the office was allocated on a random basis. There were three of us who took it in turns to be duty manager, one week at a time, so we were on call to attend any client requiring our executive exclusive services. This could be straightforward, or complicated, or maybe simply holding someone's hands. Saturday attendances were quite frequent, as if you knew where to go it was usually possible to obtain the correct documentation, except for those issued by the local registrar's office. They wouldn't open for anyone.

The country of Greece has many families connected with the shipping industry, not just those well known such as Onassis and Livornos. These are the ones who are maybe just as wealthy, but shun publicity. Such was the family I made repatriations for. There was only one thing that made this particular occasion stand out from the thousands of others. The senior lady of the house was waiting for me in her 1920s Knightsbridge apartment. It was the top floor, with a concierge service to screen callers, when I arrived a solid wooden door was opened by the lady, no servants, just her. The corridor was long and narrow, she walked, I followed. Half way down, I stopped, as my attention was arrested by a painting at eye level on the left side. It was one of the Sunflowers.

It was completely unguarded, no protection, no strip light over the top, no glass, just natural light from an open door so I could see better. My mouth must have been open, because she saw I wasn't following and returned to my side.

'Is that?…' I asked.

Very matter-of-fact 'Oh yes'.

For her, having a masterpiece on display was completely natural, nothing unusual, so I can only assume that the majority of her visitors were close friends who would not have been fazed in any way by seeing painting perfection so close, without the museum rope in the way. This was the most amazing thing that ever occurred to me, and there were many others while working in that office. All these years later I can still be there, run through the sequence in my mind, still seeing the 'Sunflowers' that no-one knows the location.

***

Another occasion had the potential to end my career as a funeral director. It had to be handled with so much tact and discretion, while all the time being on public view.

It didn't take long to know which planes were suitable for transporting coffins. If they were too small, it just wasn't going to happen, because the design of a 12 seater jet is quite straightforward. You walk up the steps, in front of you are the galley and toilet, if you turn left there is a curtain, behind which are the seats for pilot and co-pilot. Turn right and there are twelve seats. Maybe at the back this is where the toilet is located, if the design of the galley is larger. The twelve seats are plush leather reclining armchairs, so without two of the seats there is no room for a coffin. That is presupposing that a coffin will turn in the narrow area at the top of the stairs, because there is no passageway, all space is carefully utilised, and a solid object like a coffin, even though it is possible to carry it up the aircraft steps, it is just not physically possible to turn it in the narrow confined space to get into the passenger seating area.

Sometimes clients have opinions that just will not be budged, even when confronted with common sense and logic, and this was one of those occasions.

The family originated from Bahrein, with the intention or repatriating their relative back to the home country for burial. For the office this was something we arranged sometimes half a dozen times a day, we were so experienced, and that was why we were so successful. We knew what we were doing. But this family just would not be told when I said that the coffin would not fit in the private jet. They were obdurate. They insisted that it would fit, it would work, it was possible. I knew that I was going to be the man on the spot that evening, about seven o'clock on a winters evening, in the private jet area between terminals one and two at Heathrow, overlooked by bored passengers, very likely with cameras, ready to send photos to The Sun and Mirror papers. I knew that I was going to have a confrontation at the bottom of the private jet's steps when the coffin would not fit. And I had to have an alternative plan, or my career was gone.

At 10pm that same evening there was a scheduled flight going to Bahrain, so I booked the coffin on this as freight, including as part of the pre-paid fees on the understanding it would be refunded to the family if not used. As per usual, I reported to the family at the bottom of the aircraft steps. It was an unpleasant rainy evening, and it was just me and the hearse driver to carry the coffin up the steps. We both walked up the stairs, and confirmed my fears. There just wasn't room to turn the coffin. It was not going to happen, but this is where the awkward situation started.

The client said 'If the coffin won't go up the steps, then we will take the body out of the coffin, and strap it into the seat.'

'Sir, regrettably, I can't allow this to happen. You must appreciate that we have various rules and regulations for the transportation of human remains, and allowing them to fly in such an unprotected way is not allowed.'

'I don't care about rules and regulations, my brother is going to be taken home in this jet, and that is that.'

'Sir, I really want to co-operate, as I appreciate how much of a distressing time this is for you. I realise that you want to do everything you can for him, but in reality I just can't allow this to occur. It has never happened before, because it is not allowed.'

This is when the pilot intervened. He was a John Voigt look-a-like, tall, blonde haired, very attractive, looking good in his navy uniform with gold braid.

'I have done it before.'

'Excuse me for asking, but would you kindly tell me the circumstances?'

'Yes, it was last year, in Paris, and we flew a body without a coffin.'

'That must have been interesting. There must have been more to the story than this. Kindly elaborate.'

'Well, we had eight passengers on board, we were on the Paris tarmac, waiting to take off, and there was an argument between two of the passengers. It was a violent one, with knives. One passenger attacked the other, killing him.'

My client was fascinated by this story as well, not having heard it before.

'What happened next?' said my client.

The pilot continued 'We were in a very difficult position, the plane was ready to go, we would have had to return, then the police, then all the other authorities, so the decision was taken to strap the body into the seat, take off, and sort it all out at the other end, which we did.'

I looked at my client. 'I think that makes my point, don't you sir. I have the coffin booked freight, so by the time that your plane arrives there is only a three hour difference, and the scheduled flight will be arriving as well. With your permission, that it what I propose to do.'

The client just nodded, the hearse driver and I got into the hearse and drove off to the cargo area, while the passengers got into the plane.

Sometimes you just have to be firm, polite, and get your own way.

***

Conducting funerals was just one of my many roles, and the office had the contract with the Ismaili Mosque in Knightsbridge. It almost always followed the same procedure.

The start time was usually 10am, so the hearse would come to the office by 9.30 to collect me. I would be dressed formally, with herringbone trousers, white shirt, black patterned tie, black waistcoat, and black tailcoat. I did not wear a top hat for these funerals, and the tailcoat would be swapped for a black raincoat in wet weather, and a thick overcoat during the winter. The funeral clothing was kept in the office to change into from my usual formal suit.

I would have all the relevant paperwork, and we would have been instructed by the man who would take the service. His name was Missionary Hajji, a very serious man in his mid 40s. He was responsible for paying the account as well, so wanted to keep the overheads down as much as possible. This meant that we did as well, so there was just me and the hearse driver as staff provided, male mourners at the mosque and burial ground would carry at all times. In a way I was superfluous, but had to be there in case of any eventuality requiring management intervention.

The hearse driver was almost always Ernie, a smart, presentable man who had been a sergeant driver in the Metropolitan Police and retired after his thirty years, then coming to Kenyons as a hearse driver. He was used to driving fast police cars, and a 4.2 litre Daimler hearse was another wonderful toy for him to manoeuvre round London traffic.

We would arrive at the mosque by 9.45am, double park outside, so at 9.57am Missionary Hajji would bring the male mourners out from the mosque. They would have already removed their shoes inside, so if it was a wet day then they suffered. No rule breaking. Up to twenty men would manhandle the coffin from the back of the hearse into the mosque, Ernie and I stood to one side and let them get on with it. We were both of the same opinion. If there were willing people to carry the coffin, then let them get on with it.

Missionary Hajji would always chant the same words, the men would always chant the same words back. Women were also in attendance, but they were always inside, never being allowed to touch the coffin. After about 15 minutes a pre-booked coach would arrive, usually the same driver, after about an hour of prayers the mosque door would open, the men would bring the coffin back out, Ernie would secure it in the back, I would sit in the seat alongside Ernie, and male family members would be allowed to sit in the two mourners seats behind, alongside the coffin on the bier. Missionary Hajji would be in the coach, and then Ernie would drive with the coach following behind to Brookwood Cemetery, near Woking, in Surrey, which usually took in the region of 45 minutes.

The coach could only get so close inside the cemetery with the narrow roads, so the men would have to walk. Missionary Hajji would lead the chanting again, the gravediggers would provide four shovels, and the male mourners would then fill in the grave. When all complete, Ernie and I would return to London. It was a matter of professional pride for Ernie to drive as quickly as possible, and he was very proud that he managed to get back into west London within 21 minutes on one memorable occasion. We travelled in excess of 110 m.p.h.

On one very funny occasion, we had a new coach driver, who hadn't been primed by his boss, so didn't know what to expect. Ernie and I had quite a rapport, both being able to keep a straight face when perhaps not quite being truthful in a blokey way. The coach driver arrived, nothing going on, so asked what to expect. I have a silly sense of humour, Ernie and I looked at each other, so without cracking I said words along the following lines.

'What's going to happen is this. The man in charge is Missionary Hajji. When the prayers have been completed, he is going to lead the men out, and they're going to place the coffin in the back of the hearse. He is going to be chanting. What he'll be chanting is "Ha ha sunni na, sunni sunni suli na".

Now, I happen to speak a bit of Arabic, so I know what he saying. He is singing, In Arabic, "Old Macdonald Had a farm". Ernie and I held it together.

'Then, they are going to chant back the same words, "Ha Ha sunni na, sunni sunni suli na". In Arabic, that is translated as "eei eei mo".

The driver looked at us, completely unsure. He got behind the wheel of his coach, waiting, and Ernie and I deliberately watched his face when the coffin and procession emerged, chanting away.

***

We would arrange any kind of funeral services both in the UK and overseas for people from a vast varieties of backgrounds. One such occasion merited the return of the Ambassador from New Zealand back to his home country, as he sadly passed away while still in office. This warranted the Home Office to be heavily involved, as it was important to show that our country takes the repatriation of dignitaries very seriously, with all protocols being observed.

The official Residence at the time was in Chelsea Square, so I arrived with hearse and driver at the appointed time. After discussing details with the person in charge, checking through their requirements, the hearse driver and I then had a very revealing chat with the police sergeant in charge of his detail.

There is a pecking order with the police motorbike attachment, the sergeant is the man who is responsible for the smooth running, and they are usually on Royal protection. Motor bike escorts are from one to five strong, depending on the security risk and importance of the Royal, so if it is the Queen, say, then she always warrants the full quota, whereas if it is to be more low profile, say on the rare occasions that the Duke of York's daughters warrant a police motorbike escort, then it would likely be one bike and one patrol car. As this was one of the most prestigious occasions where show was the maximum importance with a very low security level, we had the full five motor bikes, together with three cars. Despite the extensive experience, this was a new one for me, so I said to the sergeant in charge

'So what happens here then? We are off to Gatwick, what route are we taking, how long will it take?'

His reply was along the lines of 'your hearse rides on my back wheel. You don't allow as much as a fag paper to get in between, and we don't stop all the way. Whatever happens, your vehicle is the important one to get through the traffic, so we will make sure that nothing gets in our way. Don't worry,' he said with a grin, 'we've done this before.'

'So your responsibility ends when we get to Gatwick?'

'Correct. When the wheels stop rolling, you've arrived, and you're on your own.'

'Looking forward to it.'

The cortege consisted of two police cars in front, then our friendly sergeant, with the other four bikes waiting idly. The hearse was next, then one limousine provided by my firm with Family, then more cars with staff and other family who would be returning in the plane for the funeral, then a couple of luggage cars, then a last police car to end the procession.

After about ten minutes we were ready to go, so off went the four extra bikes, leap-frogging each other at every junction, holding up the traffic, whistles blowing to gain attention, then when we were past riding off again in front. Quite a procedure, but it meant that we kept a steady 30 mph in London traffic, which included Wandsworth High Street. Now I don't know if you are familiar with this infamous bottleneck, but it is notorious for adding on unnecessary time to the travel time. Not this time. We did not stop. Not for roundabouts, a drive-through McDonalds, red traffic lights, pedestrian crossings, traffic in the way mysteriously disappeared. This was the way to travel!

Very soon we were on the three lane section of the A3, which was when it continued to be very interesting. The extra motor bikes were not necessary to stop traffic at junctions, but two were at the front with the cars to clear traffic out the way, and two were at the rear with a car, straddling all lanes, so nothing could overtake, with the whole procession serenely moseying on down to Gatwick at a steady 50mph. No other vehicles in sight, they had all sped away in front, nothing behind, they couldn't get past. Believe me when I say it was the fastest and smoothest journeys to Gatwick I have ever undertaken, and all my years I know I have been there over ten thousand times. Simply the best journey of the lot.

All too soon we were at the North Terminal private section, where representatives of the Foreign Office were waiting for us. I recognised a couple of political ministers, there must have been a couple of dozen of them there, just standing around, waiting, not knowing what to do next. It was a coffin, so they didn't want to be seen to be insensitive, ordering people what to do in case it was a the wrong thing. I took control.

We drove to the bottom of the aircraft steps, with the head of the airport cargo section standing in front of his team of men. It was a lovely day fortunately, no rain, but they were all afflicted with the same malaise. Don't know what to do.

I had all the correct documentation and accreditation to accompany the coffin, which was minimal due to the fact that as a serving diplomat he had immunity, so in front of all the Foreign Office dignitaries, the Family, and waiting Police, I said to the cargo chief

'whereabouts in the plane is the coffin going to go? Is it the cargo hold as usual?'

'where do you think is best?'

I turned to the Family. 'If I may, I will give you some advice. As the plane journey is a very long one, it is going to be distressing for you if the coffin is placed in the main passenger section of the aircraft. In any case it is very rare for the coffin to travel in this way, so with your approval I will organise for it to be placed securely and with dignity in the lower section of the plane, so when you ultimately arrive home it can be safely and with dignity transported to your final destination.'

'Yes please, kindly arrange.'

'Certainly madam, just leave it with me while you freshen up and take advantage of the facilities the airport has to offer.'

I then turned round to the cargo chief, looked at the conveyor belt that went up to the cargo area. I suggested to him that a couple of his men went up into the hold, my hearse driver and myself placed the coffin on the belt. Up it went into the hold, all was discreetly handled and conducted, everyone was satisfied, professional job completed.

Lesson to be learned? Just because it is an important occasion, never lose sight of the fact that people still need to be told what to do. Take control, make sure you get your own way, and all will be well. This stood me in good stead for all my career as a high-profile funeral director.

***

One of the most memorable funerals I ever conducted occurred on a Saturday morning. Working in the overseas office as I am sure you will already have gathered was an interesting place to be, often being available at short notice and odd hours. Saturday funerals are rare, with a financial premium putting off the majority of mourning families. However, when the monetary source comes from crime, being cash and limitless, then what they want happens.

A gentleman involved in a North West London crime family had met a sudden end, so a show occasion had to be arranged. They had ordered a 14 gauge metal casket, with a split lid for viewing, with the funeral arranged into quite a few sections. The first was to meet at the venue for the public displaying of the casket. Praed Street Paddington was a one way street, sufficiently wide for many buses, lots of heavy traffic, and the venue was close and on the opposite side of the street to St. Mary's Hospital.

There was a long terrace of shops and businesses on the south side of the street, deep basements, one of which was the venue for a seedy club. The entrance doorway was quite wide certainly big enough to accommodate two bouncers standing shoulder to shoulder every evening, so they were opened wide for my team of six men to stagger through and down the stairs under the burden of the very heavy metal casket. These men were all on an excellent overtime rate from start to finish, so were in no rush to hurry proceedings even if they had been able to. I had already been downstairs to check the layout, discussing in detail with the chief mourners exactly what was feasible and what was not. All their instructions could fortunately be completed to their satisfaction.

The club had a large bar against a side wall, but the main feature of the room was the small stage. It was raised by about three feet, only long enough for six showgirls to stand shoulder to shoulder, not that there were any showgirls present that I could see, and deep to the rear wall the stage was set by a further four foot. There was a side curtain to the rear 'dressing' room, so when my team manhandled the casket down the stairs wooden trestles were waiting on the stage. These were covered in a velvet material so the bare wood was not evident, making them appear suitable to rest the casket on. They were sturdy and wide, because the casket base was four foot across. There could be no possibility of imbalance, because when the lid was raised, its weight could take the whole of the casket weight back with it if the funeral staff were sufficiently inexperienced to anticipate.

We balanced the casket just right, and withdrew to the back of the room. I am not being fanciful when I say that between me and my team we reckoned that every villain in London was there to show their respects. Our company was frequently used for these occasions, we certainly didn't socialise, but we knew who they were, they knew who we were, and they greatly respected our professionalism and tact when they required our services. Some years later when I owned Cheam Limousines Toby von Judge was a very good friend and client. Toby is well worth Googling in to learn more about London's underside, an interesting and fascinating man who knew the Kray family well.

The timing of these occasions is crucial, we had a schedule to keep, one hour had been allowed for at this club. While all this was occurring, Praed Street's five lanes had been restricted to just two, with three outside the club double and triple parking with flashy mobster motors and men in dark suits and sunglasses staring at everyone, daring them to object. No traffic wardens, they would very likely have been bought off to stay away.

After an hour I approached the chief mourner, asking if it was in order to proceed. When he affirmed, my team went forward, lowered the lid, sealed it, and then with as much dignity as possible carried the casket up the reasonably narrow stairs to the waiting hearse. I waited for ten minutes as all arrived through the doorway into the waiting sunlight, then got in their waiting fleet. It is easy to exaggerate in a situation like this, but afterwards when my team discussed the flashiness of the occasion, it was generally reckoned that there were well over fifty vehicles in the cortege, and it could have been one hundred. I walked in front of the hearse to the first junction, waiting for the traffic lights to turn favourable. My top hat was carried in my right hand, I was wearing my full funeral uniform, it must have made an impressive sight as we set off on our Saturday morning jaunt.

The men driving the following vehicles were all professionals, they were on each others' bumpers straight away, no-one could possibly get in between the whole fleet, once the lights went green, it made no difference what colour they subsequently turned, the cars followed. After five minutes of walking, I paused, bowed to the hearse and casket, then got in the front seat alongside the driver. We were off, never travelling at more than 20 mph. When the cortege arrived at the southern end of Park Lane, just before the Hilton Hotel, we turned left alongside the Playboy Club. This was my cue to get out and walk again, because waiting for us was a ten piece New Orleans jazz band. They played us into Piccadilly, where we turned right to Hyde Park Corner, we walked all along this route, playing an assortment of tunes, such as 'When The Saints Go Marching In', then north into Park Lane again, where the band stopped playing, I got back into the hearse, so off we went to Golders Green Crematorium. After committal, the casket was discarded because it could not be cremated, so another cheaper wooden casket was waiting and used.

This funeral was mentioned many times on Capital Radio that morning. Avoid the area, massive traffic jams. Such power.

***

There was another hearse driver, even more experienced, whose name was Harold Longhurst. Harold had been with the company for many years, and was the senior hearse driver through merit as well as seniority. He was a professional through and through, lovely sense of humour, so I feel privileged to have known Harold. He was a crafty old bugger as well. There are usually four men to carry a coffin, normally matching height, and he was well known in his later professional years to bend his knees slightly so he carried less weight, increasing the burden of his colleagues. Afterwards, he was also well known to say with a wry smile 'that was all there, wasn't it?' as if he had done his bit.

This particular incident occurred in Harold's last year, as he retired at 65. The office had a funeral to take at Oxford Crematorium, just over an hours' drive west of London. There were just the two of us in the hearse, as we hired three local Oxford bearers. We took the A40 road, and were about twenty minutes from our destination when Harold uttered the words every funeral director dreads to hear.

'We have got a problem'.

It was a flat tyre, the rear one on the passenger side, so there was nothing for it but to pull to the side of the road. I was in my late 30s at the time, Harold was 64, so there was no other option but for me to change the wheel. Off came the jacket, up went the pure white shirt sleeves, out came the jack, under the hearse I went to fit it, wheel changed, twenty minutes later all complete, but now I was dirty. No problem, Harold being the old school professional that he was, he went under the bier and came out with soap, water, and hand towels. Suitably clean, I dressed back to previous presentation, so we carried on as if there had been no problem, no-one any the wiser.

This had occurred on the Friday, so on Monday morning I was walking across the garage floor when Harold called me over. 'Harry, Harry, come over here.' He was chatting to at least half a dozen of the other drivers.

The one sided conversation went like this.

Harold: Harry, did we go somewhere last Friday?
Me: Yes, Oxford.
Harold: Did we have a problem?
Me: Not really, except for the puncture
Harold: who changed the wheel?
Me: me
Harold: How long did it take you?
Me: about twenty minutes

Harold: Did you watch the Grand Prix yesterday?
Me: Yes
Harold: Did they change any wheels?
Me: Yes, four
Harold: How long did they take?
Me: Less than ten seconds
Harold: How long did you take to change just one?
The men collapsed with laughter

When a few months later, dear Harold finally retired after many years of loyal employment, the firm held a leaving party for him. One of the directors was a man called John Sheldon, who should have retired a long time previously, but because of his shareholding and other factors was still hanging in there. He was a very patronising man, he had been a funeral director for many tens of years, owning a London firm that had been purchased some years previously, thereby gaining his importance. It was him we listened to when he gave Harold's farewell speech. It contained a memorable sentence I can remember word for word. This sentence typified the way that the firm looked at its staff, with those fortunate enough to gain importance looking down on those lowly serfs fortunate to have a job. The sentence John Sheldon said was 'I don't know where we are going to find servants like Harold in future'.

***

We made all funeral arrangements for people of a celebrity background, and one such occasion was when Felicity Kendall lost her sister Jennifer Kapoor, who was married to the Indian movie director Ravi.

Miss Kendall did not come into the office, which was a great disappointment to Phil, the office manager. He was a great fan of this famous actress, but Phil almost always confined his professional activities inside the office, as he was better able to control the smooth running of this complex operation. It was a very rare occasion for Phil to venture outside, leaving visits to others. Less than half the clients actually ventured into the office, as all arrangements could quite easily be made without bothering, our clients were wealthy and busy people who were used to services being provided for their convenience.

The house visit was made by a colleague, so I did not meet Miss Kendall at any stage. However, this didn't mean that there was some mileage to be exploited with a vulnerable colleague when I could indulge in my silly sense of humour. I would also say that the actress was never aware of what subsequently occurred, and if she ever gets to read or hear of this incident, hope that she sees the humour of the situation, rather than any degree of unprofessionalism or bad taste.

Phil was a lovely chap, extremely efficient at his job, over six feet tall, slim, fit, almost a workaholic, and someone who shunned the limelight while enjoying show business connections. He was ripe for a prank.

In the mid-1980s, a lot of communications were transmitted by fax, or a tickertape machine. This device received messages on a long strip of paper, had a keypad like a QWERTY so the words could be written by the sender, and the message received on another machine with holes that could be easily read. The taped message could be composed first, ensuring accuracy, and then the send button pressed. Each machine had its own identity code, so the receiver could ensure the veracity. But I got round this by composing my message, and then getting a friend to send from his machine. Yes, there was a code, but it was a difficult one to identify, and if the recipient really wanted to believe the message, then they would not doubt it at all. My message to Phil went like this.

HI THERE. WE ARE TRANS-GLOBAL PRODUCTIONS IN L.A., CALIFORNIA, AND THIS IS THE LONDON U.K. OFFICE. WE HAVE A MOVIE PLANNED STARRING FRANK SINATRA, MARLON BRANDO, SOPHIA LOREN AND FELICITY KENDALL. ONE SCENE HAS A FUNERAL AND WE NEED AN ADVISOR. YOUR NAME MR. HARRIS HAS BEEN

GIVEN TO US AS AN EXPERT, AND WE WOULD LIKE TO OFFER YOU TEN THOUSAND DOLLARS FOR ONE MONTH ALL EXPENSES PAID IN L.A. PLEASE RING HOLLYWOOD 718 6358 IF YOU ARE AVAILABLE.

Phil was really excited, he could barely contain himself, and rang the company chairman Michael Kenyon to ask for the time off. The boss asked why, asking Phil if he had been able to get through to Trans Global Productions. Phil replied that he had a little temporary difficulty, and the advice was to wait a little while before actually taking the time off.

I was out of the office while this phone conversation occurred, and when I got back Phil took one look at me and a red mist descended. I legged it. I was gone. Chiltern Street is one way, and I ran faster than the traffic with him trying to catch up. No good, I couldn't run any more, I was laughing so much, I turned to face him, and we both stood in the middle of the street, roaring our heads off.

***

One of the reasons why Kenyons was such a prestigious company to work for at that time was because they had something called the air crash team. That was instructed by the authorities should there be a disaster anywhere in the world involving British nationals – or sometimes not. Its full title was Kenyon Emergency Services.

I was on that team all during my Kenyon employment, so it was a very interesting period in my professional life, because among the disasters I was involved with were Air India in the Irish Sea, The Herald of Free Enterprise ferry, The Marchioness pleasure boat in the River Thames, the Piper Alpha oil rig, and the most memorable of all, the Lockerbie Pan Am plane crash.

Various company main board directors were involved with the air crash team, but we had a specific level of responsibility. As a KAT operative, I was under John Nicholls, Albert Cook and Christopher Kenyon; the first two of these were legends in the business, John giving lectures world-wide.

He was a great ambassador, gruff voiced, always suited, the voice of experience. John was the epitome of how the profession should be presented – a mature man who was prepared to share his experience, passing on his wealth of knowledge to eager minds, while maintaining the air of mystery surrounding such a complex subject. I am pretty certain that he had been a funeral director over the years, coming into this speciality due to being in the right place at the right time. John also had to be firm in very difficult circumstances, when being pressed to do things by suddenly bereaved families that were just not on. A prime example was the Air India disaster in 1985.

This was my first hands on experience of being involved with a disaster of this magnitude, being based at the London office and then attending the air crash room in head office out of office hours. The hours were onerous, the tasks requiring a great deal of tact, and we were not paid any extra, because we were management and expected to perform extra tasks when required.

On 23rd June Air India flight 182 was en route from Toronto and Montreal in Canada, stopping in London, then on to Delhi, with 329 people on board. Due to a bomb exploding while over Irish air space, all those on board perished. While only 24 passengers were registered as from India, a large number had strong connections with this country, with the majority being recognised as Canadian citizens with Indian descent.

It took a few days to locate the aircraft on the Irish sea bed, which gave us in the office a little time to prepare ourselves. It was to be my first experience of a major disaster, so despite the seriousness of the occasion human nature being what it is I was intrigued as to what to expect, and what my role would be. The main board room of Kenyons was at their Freston Road garage in West London, garage premises, mortuary, offices, administration, no facility to arrange funerals as no public were usually admitted. It was quite a conventional layout for a building of this nature, the freehold owned by the company. It was a very short walk from the local tube station, the road ending just beyond the premises due to the railway lines. The main garage entrance was on the right side of the building, going back a long way to accommodate at least a dozen funeral vehicles, the embalming room at the back, workshop the otherwise. Offices were upstairs, which is also where the Muslim preparation rooms were located. The directors' offices were also on this floor, and it was here that I reported every evening after work. My role was a simple but functionary one. I answered the phone, fielding calls, and operated the telex machine. We had white boards on the walls to aid identification purposes, because we were the home team. The main hands on operation was in an aircraft hangar on the Irish west coast, close to a port, so when the bodies and possessions were brought in, they could be categorised with the minimum of fuss, the maximum of professionalism, and dignity could be maintained as much as possible. These hangars were inevitably cold and unwelcoming places, because despite the fact that they were temporary mortuary facilities, due to the large number they would have to be embalmed as soon as possible. Bear in mind it was June, so the preservation process had to be started as soon as possible.

As well as all these handicaps that the Kenyon staff were working under, they also had to liaise with the air crash investigators, and local coroners authority so the bodies could be identified and returned to families as soon as possible, the press, and the worst people of the lot, the families. They were vociferous, distressed, and blaming everyone to hand for the disaster. It made no difference that the people in the hangar were doing their best to maintain their dignity and professionalism under extremely trying circumstances, all they were interested in was having their relatives returned to them. Part of their religion meant that some senior male members of the family had to fast until the funeral had been held, human nature being what it is they were very hungry, they were angry, and they saw that anyone in authority was delaying their ability to have their farewells to their family member. Therefore, on a lot of occasions, there were many people all claiming that a particular deceased they were viewing belonged to them, they wanted the body, and then they could have their funeral.

The bodies were being recovered from the wreckage a few at a time, so when word went round the identification village there was a mass of relatives demanding to view so they could successfully identify. Unfortunately, only 132 bodies were ever recovered, and there were a lot of very unhappy families without a funeral.

My role, as I said, was an office one in the home office of the air crash team, in the first five or six days there were half a dozen of us all the time, with a director to take the most difficult calls, and one person stayed in the room all night to answer international calls, which was me for two nights. There was a temporary camp bed, and I did get some sleep both nights, despite answering a lot of phone calls and using the telex and fax machines. Of course, I didn't get to see my family on these occasions, reporting for office duties the next morning after breakfast, having a change of clothing including shirt in my office locker.

After a week of intense activity, all settled down, the hangar only had one embalmer and one office administrator, the pair staying for a month until it was calculated that all the bodies had been recovered that were going to be.

***

Townsend Thoresen owned a ferry called the Herald of Free Enterprise. She was a ro-ro ferry, which means that when you drive on at the back, you drive off the front when the doors have opened. Unfortunately, the rear doors were not sufficiently secured when she left Zeebrugge harbour in Belgium, so when she found the first good sized wave, water filled inside, creating an imbalance, and she sank very close to shore, with the resultant loss of 193 passengers and crew. This occurred on the night of 6th March 1987.

By this stage I was a very experienced funeral operator, having gained an excellent company reputation for keeping cool under pressure, and was a man on the move inside the most prestigious funeral company of them all.

The sinking of the ferry was international news, the vast majority of passengers and crew were British nationals, and so I went into the office early the next morning, fully expecting not to see my family for the next few days. This was to be the case.

As part of my Kenyon Air Transportation duties, I had to accompany and transport bodies and coffins into Europe, maybe driving the hearse, perhaps the funeral van, sometimes on my own, maybe with a driver to accompany. I did this many times, so would not have been surprised had I been delegated to the identification team in Belgium, but the powers that be decided my worth was better valued on the home team, probably because of the responsibilities I had in the office, conducting the funerals, escorting families. On reflection, I am rather glad that I did not go to Belgium, because those lads had a pretty difficult time of it, poor accommodation and diet, with the last of the team returning a couple of months later.

The pressure was intense from the very start, ferry disasters were unheard of, as well as the bodies to be identified there were the vehicles to be moved, windows had been blown out, the retrieval was going to be a protracted process, ultimately becoming more uncomfortable as time progressed as inevitably the bodies would deteriorate in the conditions.

The administration procedure continued as before. Between the Air India plane crash and now, there had been three or four minor disasters where Kenyons had been involved, less than a dozen casualties, and these experiences had stood me in good stead for the sudden catapult into the spotlight. Believe me, we were thrust right into it.

Every word was disseminated by people on the other end of the phone, asking direct questions that usually had the reply of 'I am really sorry, but I have not been given that information.' It was a very sensitive situation, with nutters ringing up as well, giving false identification, trying to trick you into giving away something that no-one else was aware of. From the very beginning, we knew the scale of the disaster, we knew who was going to be on our teams, we knew where they were working, we knew where they were staying, we knew where they were eating, all they wanted to do was get on with their jobs, not to be asked questions by people who had no business asking, so we just had to be as very careful as possible, being discreet at all times.

The press were the worst of the lot, no sensitivity at all, voyeurism and sensationalism so they could sell more papers to their voracious readers. Of course, families were liaising with identification authorities such as the Belgian coroner, but they couldn't get through a lot of the time, so were ringing us as we had a helpline. A couple of days after the disaster, families were taken to the Belgian site, but not all chose to go. Again, we used the white boards, so each victim could be named, then placed in a coffin after embalming, then released to families for the funeral, but all this inevitably took a lot of time. It is not until you are actively involved in a disaster of this magnitude that you appreciate the care and concern that goes into the successful identification of each body, so when you have 193 families then pressure is greater than you can possibly conceive.

A very strange thing occurred during this disaster, one that has never gained any publicity at all, I have an idea that no-one has ever mentioned it since, but it is something that was discussed among the Kenyon staff at the time, and one that has never been resolved to my satisfaction. It probably never will.

There was an extra English car in the vehicle part of the ferry, and the manifest gave it as being owned by a man in the English Army. He was stationed in Germany, and was returning to the UK on disciplinary charges, very likely going to be dishonourably discharged. The ignominy he was returning to was going to be great, but he had no escort as he was travelling under his own recognizance and honour. The car was there, but his body was never found. His was the only body never recovered, and there was some supposition that he swam ashore, and simply disappeared.

True or apocryphal? No idea, just repeating what was said at the time.

***

Occidental Petroleum owned an oil rig in the North Sea, and on the 6th July 1988 there was a huge explosion, which resulted in

167 fatalities. We were placed on standby, but I had very little involvement on this occasion.

I had been with the company for four years by this time, with my duties taking me away from the overseas office of KAT and into the administration office. This meant that I was in charge of the control room of the company, responsible for fourteen London offices, two garages, almost fifty staff, and three thousand London funerals annually. Despite theoretically being on the team, available as back-up, my role was more of as observer. As it happened, this was, strangely, one of the lower key operations that Kenyon Emergency Services to be involved in. Yes, there were a lot of fatalities, but because of the location of the oil rig, the disaster site was a long way into the North Sea, so the bodies were inaccessible.

Only a basic team were despatched to Aberdeen, after a couple of months stood down, until the accommodation platform was recovered much later on in the year, I seem to recall close to December. The other problem was the fact that the oil rig was still ablaze, despite most of it disintegrating and sinking, it was to be three weeks after the disaster until the famous Texan trouble shooter Red Adair was able to extinguish the flames. This meant that despite the best will in the world for the bodies to be identified and returned to families, very few initially were recovered. That meant that the air crash team were standing around a lot of the time waiting instructions, so it wasn't too long before they were stood down, only returning when there was something concrete for them to do.

Of course, this was a very distressing period for families who had lost their men, psychologically they were to find this period of their lives exceedingly difficult, with subsequent studies of the aftermath documenting how they coped with such trauma. Impossible to comprehend until you have experienced.

When the accommodation section was ultimately recovered, those poor men had numbered approximately 100, but there were only 87 bodies identified. The Kenyon staff returned for this process, embalming and identifying, and it must have been pretty harrowing for them as well. And then, the same year, just before Christmas, Pan Am flight 103 exploded over Lockerbie in Scotland.

***

Flight 103 was a regular daily flight from Frankfurt in Germany to Detroit in the USA, calling via London and New York. There were 243 passengers and 16 crew on the section from London to New York, but unfortunately the bomb went off as it was flying over Lockerbie, close to the Scottish Borders region. The debris covered a huge area, but where it was concentrated over civilisation there were eleven fatalities, making the death toll 270. Kenyons were immediately instructed. This time my role had to be a more active one, and it was to be a deserted Christmas in my household that year.

Because of where the disaster occurred, over land and easily accessible, it meant that the recovery process was going to be a lot more straightforward than on some of the more difficult occasions.

The air crash emergency team had grown considerably by this time, because the company directors had appreciated that there was an increasing likelihood that there was going to be a larger disaster, liaising with all authorities, bringing their vast experience and influence to aid the planning. This meant that Kenyons had to anticipate by training more operatives in the field, so there were increasing weekends where funeral professionals including embalmers with vast experience and years of expertise in problematic situations could be available for just this eventuality. This forethought was to prove invaluable, as the procedures in the Lockerbie area were able to be completed with professionalism and dignity, something that might not necessarily have occurred five years previously with such a large number of fatalities.

Because a large number of passengers came from the USA, 189, and a lot of them were relatively young, there was a lot of intense pressure exerted on apportioning blame. We were there, answering questions, and if we were not being as forthcoming with information as vociferous grieving families required, then we were there to be vilified. That occurred a lot on the phone, and with the others I had to exercise a lot of tact and discretion. I remember one particular grieving father who became a spokesman for a lot of others was particularly unpleasant and difficult to deal with. He was completely focused in his grief, if you couldn't help him, then he was against you. He wanted to know everything, it soon became obvious that this was going to be a precursor to litigation, every comment would be disseminated, and I was by now a senior member of staff, one level away from the main board of directors with the resultant experience and responsibility, it was inevitable that other team members would refer to me for guidance.

The press were on the phone to us all the time, and so were the aforementioned nutters, you know, the ones that find satisfaction from being aware and involved. We had one idiot in the garage who was a driver and when the Marchioness sank in the River Thames the following year, heard about it on the media and immediately turned up on site, loudly proclaiming that he worked for the funeral directors who would be identifying the bodies and he was prepared to remove his jacket and start working there and then. It was my job to have the satisfaction of terminating his employment. My, but there were some good aspects to the job.

The first few days of a disaster are usually the most intense, but company chairman Michael Kenyon appreciated that even though those in Lockerbie could not be spared, the home team could be wound down, so as long as there was one person to man the office at all times of the day and night, some could be spared so they could spend time with their families. I managed to get away on a couple of occasions like that, and later on in January Michael was very kind to discreetly give me an envelope containing £100 in cash as a bonus and appreciation of efforts.

Pretty early on communications had improved, so we were able to liaise with the field team, being privy to facts not widely known, so caution was essential. The recovery process was fast and efficient, so after less than a month the vast majority of local personnel were stood down. The staff rotation was very efficient, quietly performed so most people were completely unaware of what my colleagues were doing. I am quite certain that nowadays this procedure has been further refined, as successive governments have appreciated that there has to be a contingency in place. That is where the Kenyon expertise was invaluable, and I am proud to have been part of it, albeit for only a few years.

***

The next episode is one that I am not particularly proud of, despite the fact that I performed with professionalism and tact. It concerned a branch in West London. The resident office manager and his wife were on holiday for a week, so a relief manager was in charge. There were to be two burial services, one on the Thursday in July 1989, the other the next day, both coincidentally preceded by Mass in the local Polish Cathedral. So far so good, but unfortunately Mark the relief manager was a lazy man, so did not check that the correct coffin was taken out for the first funeral on the Thursday. The Friday coffin was taken out instead.

It is very easy to criticise, but if you are distracted for example by being on the phone, or arranging another funeral as you were in the branch on your own, then the staff can enter, assume they have the correct one because the flowers are on top, thereby hiding the identifying inscription plate. The men can be on their way by the time you realise that an error has occurred. I am not attempting to condone Mark's actions, because to this day I feel highly aggrieved at his actions and the subsequent decisions made by higher management. I sit here recounting this story all these years later still highly upset that firstly an error of this magnitude occurred, and secondly it was covered up to save blushes.

Mark allowed the first funeral to continue, despite knowing they had the incorrect body. He just hoped that nothing would be discovered. To compound his calumny, he then ordered another coffin plate for the second funeral, so it could be swapped onto the Thursday coffin, thereby a second funeral would occur with the incorrect body.

He must have approached the Friday morning with a high degree of trepidation, knowing he was going to do something so morally and socially unacceptable, as well as illegal with a custodial sentence a likely outcome. But Mark allowed that second funeral to occur.

I never discovered how his actions were discovered, but suspect that alarm bells were rung when the workshop were asked to prepare a substitute coffin plate at very short notice when records would show that there was no error on the first one. As area manager I only found out about it when my director came to me with the details, then delegating me with the task of discreetly resolving so there would be no publicity or prosecutions. At all costs the company reputation must be unsullied, as at that time we were still funeral directors for the Royal Family.

My first response was to visit the Priest in charge of the Catholic Cathedral. My conversation to the stony faced priest went along these lines:

'Father, my company has made a monumental error, one that we want to resolve with as little distress as possible. Our relief branch manager has allowed two funerals yesterday and today to be completed with the wrong coffins being buried in the wrong graves. It has only come to light now, and I have immediately come round to ask your indulgence, compassion, and assistance in righting such a heinous wrong that is so unforgivable and almost impossible to imagine.'

The Polish Priest replied 'What do you want me to do?' This was said in a very stern, disapproving manner, it was obvious he found the whole episode distasteful and did not want any part of it, being dragged in against his wishes.

'My suggestion Father is that I have my car outside, and I drive you to each family's house. I then explain what we have done, tell them that we will do everything in our power to carry out their wishes whatever they may be, without any consideration for expense, and do my best to show the families that as a company we take this sort of error with the utmost seriousness.'

To my relief, he concurred, went into a back room so he could change into suitable attire – is there ever any suitable attire for this kind of occasion – and then we were in the car to the first family's home. Of course, they were surprised to find a priest and funeral director on their doorstep the day after their male family member's burial, inviting us in with curiosity. We were sat in the front parlour, me, the priest, the widow, her two sons and one daughter, only slightly relaxing after the traumas of the previous day. This is where my presence of mind having the priest sat next to me became very wise, because there was an absolute certainty that these two sensitive sons were going to inflict some serious damage on me, as the representative, but they couldn't possibly do this with the Father sitting next to me.

The family were also Polish, so I had to explain very slowly and clearly what had occurred. Repeating my regret that we were there in their lounge explaining what a monumental error our company representative had allowed to happen. I explained the consequences, that the Priest and me would be visiting the other family, and it might be a good idea if they were to communicate with each other once the news had sunk in that they were visiting the wrong coffin in the correct grave. If both families wanted, we would arrange for both to be exhumed and then re-buried in the correct cemetery. There would be no cost. The previous day's funeral service would not have an account. And when they ultimately decided on what cemetery outcome both families wanted, there would be no charge for headstone and monumental tributes. All costs would be met by the company. I also said that of course news of this magnitude would need a few days to take in, so with the Priest's permission we would go and see the other family and break the sad news to them as well.

Of course, they were completely stunned, but I could see real anger on the faces of the two sons and one daughter, they were almost beside themselves with fury. However, I did not rush my exit, assured them instead that I would do everything in my power to ensure that whatever wishes they had were completed. I would be their liaison with the Cathedral, so if they didn't want anything more to do with me, I understood. I never saw them again.

The next visit was even more difficult, because their grief was even more raw, the news was even more sensitive to share.

The family gathering was larger, everyone wanted to know why the Priest and undertaker were visiting, and they had already consumed quite large quantities of alcohol. I was clear headed, took a deep breath, and started explaining. The widow had a poor understanding of English, so the Father had to translate every sentence for me. While giving me extra time to gather my thoughts for the next sentence, it also gave the male members more time to hear first in English and then in Polish what had occurred. I knew that I was going to have to be very careful to ensure a safe exit from this house. They were shouting and exclaiming loudly, but the surprising thing was the widow was the calming influence, realising very quickly that it just wasn't my direct fault, I had nothing to do with it, I was there to resolve, to admit responsibility, and try to make the best of an impossible situation. That was my salvation. I was never to see this family again either.

The couple responsible for the normal smooth running of this highly efficient office returned from their holiday the following Monday, immediately contacted the cathedral, and were able to smooth as well as they could, but of course I was aware of what was occurring from behind the scenes.

I left the priest at the second house with his permission, the widow even taking my hands in hers in a very understanding and sympathetic way. I then returned to my boss's office, as he was waiting to hear what had been resolved.

By this time it was early on the Friday evening, about seven pm, we were alone in his office, the mood though serious was initially relaxed because I told him about the way that it had been accepted initially by both families, they accepted that we had erred and wanted to atone immediately, and there would be no publicity. They would not be reporting the matter to the authorities, there would be no prosecution, the company would not be fined. We then came to what was going to happen to Mark.

My boss informed me that nothing was going to happen, it was going to be brushed under the carpet. I was simply astounded. Had I gone through all that anguish, resolved everything so well, all so that revolting creep could get away with it. All he could do was wring his hands in a very weak ineffective way. I seem to remember telling him what I thought of him as a man, as a boss, as a person, as a weak worm without spine, backbone, a creep. I was incensed. I choose not to identify him now purely because I consider it to be the correct thing to do.

He then calmly explained that the company could not afford any publicity of any nature because we were in the process of being taken over by a larger outfit from the Midlands, and any adverse news would affect the sensitivities of the situation. That made me explode all the more, accusing my boss of allowing these circumstances to overcome what is decent and the principles the company stood for. I told him that it was going to be Mark or me. He had to decide, there and then, because I didn't want to work for a firm that would allow its traditions to be destroyed in such a way. I was shouting at him, he was using all the tact he could to calm me down. He explained that he didn't want to lose me, he would do everything in his power to sort Mark out later, it was just not expedient to do it now. This is where to my shame I capitulated. I calmed down, saw the bigger picture, so Mark was suspended for three months without pay, with re-training when he returned. My only lapse in memory of all of this is Mark's surname, because believe me if I could recall then his full name would feature heavily.

The news broke in the press that weekend that Kenyons were being taken over by a Birmingham funeral director, who was a complex character, a reputation for ruthlessness, and the Royal undertakers were now in the hands of a very different class of person. Gentlemen became commoners.

***

Kenyons had principles. These meant that profit was not the ultimate aim, as they were gentlemen with traditions, then they were also vulnerable to the predator. Their profit margin was in the region of 10-11%, but the new owners was closer to 23%. He had investment banking money as backing, so was buying up everything he could, attempting to gain a monopoly in the funeral profession. Money men saw this as a good thing, reducing overheads, spreading the liabilities, traditionalists saw it from a different viewpoint.

He was dictatorial, running the business as an empire with only one ruler. This had worked for him, with a mercurial progress that was the envy of a lot of his peers. In a way, they saw him as a saviour, with a moribund funeral profession desperately in need of a new way of approaching tradition. He had been born into the profession, somewhat undistinguished until he took over the running of the family firm at quite a young age. He was extremely personable, blonde hair cut in a long style, attractive, able to converse at length on his chosen subject – himself.

During his astronomic progress he had surrounded himself with a coterie of people he could trust, those who were prepared to get their hands dirty in the mundane task of running the empire under his direct orders. One such man was hatchet Harvey. Again, memory fails me so I can't recall his name, it would immediately return if you were to tell me. He was to be my ultimate boss, as he was not a main board company director.

The career problem as I saw it was I was too high in the chain, but not sufficiently high from the previous regime. Yes, I might have some support from previous Kenyon directors, but that counted for nothing with a man like Harvey. He had a reputation for complete ruthlessness, was devoted to his boss, had his ear, wanted nothing but to serve his master 24 hours a day 7 days a week. He would be given a task, such as trouble shooting the Kenyon previous empire. Save money, cut costs, trim the deadwood, get rid of anyone who had any form of independent thought. My days were doomed.

It was a hostile takeover, because of lack of financial planning the Kenyon company had been vulnerable and susceptible to another company being in the ascendancy. This was despite the fact that Kenyons were the more respectable, and much larger in the south of England. The other company base was in the Midlands, in Birmingham, spreading further north, so my company represented a real coup, especially one with such tradition and prestige. That is another reason why it had been important to bury (excuse the pun) the illegal interments.

Harvey moved into my offices immediately, the Kenyon directors were ousted, I was moved into the administration offices in a ground floor cubbyhole. The atmosphere was immediately a reign of terror, who was going to be the first to go. But my, they were subtle, very clever, especially with the way they divided key personnel. They made my old boss the regional director.

I seem to recall there were seven or eight of these, all men, mainly from larger funeral homes previously taken over. My old colleague came to hate and dread the area meetings, which were conference calls on the phone. The CEO would be in his Birmingham head office, while for at least an hour the others would be sitting by their phones around the country, being told what to do in shouting, stringent ways. His favourite was to take off a shoe and bang it on his desk, Khrushchev style, if underlings refused to immediately agree with his ramblings. Maybe I was glad that I had not been 'promoted' to this position. Let's face it, my old boss was ideally suited after his experience as a Kenyon director.

My employment managed to last until early December, I still had responsibility for the running of my depot despite the interference of Harvey and his fellow hatchet men. I even had a company car, albeit it a ten year old one that frequently broke down, my salary was the same, it was just the fact that I was working for a company I had no concern for because of their lack of standards and obsession with profitability. All new edicts involved saving money.

The first weekend of December had the tradition of being a break at the NEC Birmingham hotel for a company conference. Our Saturday night accommodation for Pam and I was paid for, but we had to pay for any additional nights. It was impractical to arrive from our South London home for a 9am Saturday start, so we stayed on the Friday night at our expenses. The conference room was huge, a raised platform had a very long table, room for a dozen bigwigs to be seated, and the central aisle at the end of the table had a focal point. A huge framed photo of our beloved leader, on an easel, probably ten feet high. It was just like a Russian, Chinese, or North Korean dictatorship, your eyes were drawn all the time away from the speaker who was spouting the company mantra to stare at him. Spooky. Each speaker banged on and on about how good the company was, how safe we were in his hands, how positive everything was, all is great. Just like in Russia, China, or North Korea. It was easy to allow the eyelids to drop, I actually saw some starting to go, the room was warm, little ventilation, a lot of heating because of the time of year, but me being the good boy that I am, managed to stay awake. What a load of company twaddle.

After a buffet lunch standing up and free of alcohol – wouldn't dare, had the afternoon session to endure – we dutifully filed back. But this was to be something different. It was the awards afternoon.

Coffin polisher of the year, hearse licker of the year, embalmer of the year (how the hell could that be judged?), all sorts of stupid awards, until we got to the area of the year. The Scots had been particularly well behaved that year, so were awarded the accolade. To the tune of Scotland the Brave on bagpipes, a dozen men came onto the stage in kilts, sporran, tam o'shanter, lucky white heather, anything else relevant to the country, and received their award. Lots of cheering, screaming, whooping, chairman very pleased with himself. Don't remember much of the rest of the afternoon, hardly surprising really, so we had to report for the formal black tie dinner just after 6pm, so it was back to rooms to change.

We were on large tables, there must have been in the region of 300 people there, all paid for by the company, and you had to be pretty strong company person to be allowed near that room. Or have a reasonably senior position like I thought I had.

After the dinner, the chairman took centre stage, with the microphone, he knew what was coming. To the repeated tune of Scotland the Brave, the dozen men in kilts trooped onto the stage, but without any warning proceeded to show their backs to the audience, then raising their kilts. They proved the myth that Scotsmen wear nothing underneath. The flash was quick, the uproar great, led by our beloved leader. He was really in his element. To more cheers, the Scotsmen then turned round, showing their full frontal to the audience. That resulted in a shocked silence. This was a formal dinner with prestigious guests from around the world, a line had been crossed. There was a further line however. The Scotsmen had arranged for a stripper gram. She was huge, in the region of thirty stones, and dressed as Mummy Christmas in a red tunic and not much else. She stripped off. Completely. The chairman was beside himself with pleasure, which increased when she found some baby oil. Mummy Christmas decided to remove his shirt, and rub some oil on his chest.

Now I am not a prude, far from it, but also I am aware of a time and a place for everything. Pam and I looked at each other, nodded, both of us got out our chairs and made for the door. Very discreetly, we hoped, but we had been seen by two of our Kenyon colleagues, who also left with us with their wives. My regional director was by the door, and as I passed him I said something along the lines of how can you stomach this sort of behaviour. His reply was along the lines of I need a job. The unspoken message was to accept this sort of situation if you want to continue in employment. I am sure if he ever reads these words he will have conveniently forgotten this incident.

The three of us were sitting in the bar with our partners when ten minutes later another of the chairman's underlings came to us and suggested it would be a good idea if we returned. I simply asked if he was still unclothed. He said yes. I then said in a very calm manner that when he learned to behave himself in public, then I would be very happy to return.

Harvey did have some decency, he wasn't the complete nasty person he attempted to be, so on Monday tried to warn me that the chairman had been aware of my departure, saw me as a ringleader, and don't be too surprised if things don't work out well for me. His advice was to keep my head down and hope for the best.

I tried to adopt this counsel, with some success as I was not bothered for quite a few weeks. But then came Friday 5th January 1990.

This was the night of the long knives, when 14 Kenyon personnel were told that their services were no longer required. I was the most senior, my old boss survived.

The way it was done was unnecessarily nasty, which was in keeping with the way that the company was being run. Three of the office personnel, myself included, were deliberately kept in seclusion on the ground floor, while one by one we were summoned to the top floor. By the time we arrived at the very top of the building, the heart was thumping in anticipation, we were out of breath, and on the back foot. All part of the psychological advantage. There were three of them sitting there, Harvey in the middle, one was a hired solicitor, the other I had never seen before and was never introduced to. Ten minutes later, six years of service counting for nothing, I was shown the door. Get out, you're fired.

And what was my annual salary on the day that I was fired? £16,000. Pretty poor, all things considered.

***

So, how did the company evolve? Hatchet Harvey survived for quite some time, ultimately being sacked (shame!), but the Kenyon group altered a lot over the subsequent years. By this time, after the acquisition, the Royal Family withdrew its patronage, which was passed to another long standing traditional family run London company.

My old boss and Michael Kenyon's son Peter were great friends, living quite close to each other, and as there was financial security with the pair they started another funeral company in the far west of London Home Counties, but I have no subsequent knowledge.

Phil Harris, who was a man of great integrity, honour and decency, survived for some time, but then left, taking all those years of experience, working for a funeral company closer to his home so he was able to appreciate family life without the business pressures. Good for him.

Various personnel who I have not named, but who came under my influence as their line manager, managed to creep their way up into the hierarchy by being perpetual yes men, have had a long and happy career, with clear consciences. John Nicholls, a man I greatly respected and admired, is apparently still alive and well although of senior age now.

The Kenyon company went through various guises over the years, and is now the premier independently quoted funeral company. They are nation-wide, enjoying a superb reputation as a respected firm.

The chairman who bought out firm out is still active in the funeral profession, running his own company. He never once looked at me in the six months I was in his senior employment, we never exchanged any words on any occasion. I was never introduced to him, but we both knew who each other was. That was his style of management, if you counted, then you were acknowledged. If you didn't, you were disposable.

So, what happened next in my life?

Well, after I was relieved of my car and career, I caught public transport home on the Friday evening. When I walked in the door with the devastating news, I hadn't touched a drop of alcohol. I dropped the bombshell, and we discussed the future. I was 42, had worked for the best company possible, there were no senior opening at any opposition nationally or locally.

I consulted a solicitor about unfair dismissal, because I was told that I would receive one weeks salary for each year I had worked for the firm. The employment legislation at the time was that if you were in receipt of a company car, then you were entitled to keep this for six months after termination of employment. That didn't happen. My solicitor thought I had a very good case, so the paperwork was prepared. The advice was to have my day in court as a last resort, because my contempt for the Kenyon personnel was so blatant that I would come across as an unsympathetic witness. Too bloody right, I wanted my day to say my piece.

Two days before the court hearing, which was scheduled for two days, and I would be the only person on my side, with a range of Kenyon personnel on the other, they offered a settlement of £10,000. I countered that I wanted this to exclude my lawyers fees, plus an extra £500 as there was something specific I wanted to indulge myself with. Of course, I had the ultimate bargaining tool in reserve – the two coffins buried in the wrong graves. They just didn't want the publicity, and I was very ready to shout about it. Their usual settlement offer was considerably less than that on the table, contemptuously in the region of doubling the minimum legal requirement. They accepted my counter offer.

By this stage, I had started my own limousine company, called Cheam Limousines. I lived in Cheam in Surrey, and had one limousine.

The cheque was received in December 1990, and the extra £500 was spent on a sound system for my car.

In May 1990 I returned to Kenyons as a sub-contractor, driving my limousine under instruction from people who had been my former colleagues under my orders. I can't have been a bad guv'nor. However, they stopped using me after the tribunal settlement under senior instructions. Pathetic, petty, and typical. Now of course it's under different ownership/management, much improved.

I expanded the business, retaining my membership of the National Association of Funeral Directors as an associate. I am very proud that I was elected Croydon area President in 1994. Cheam Limousines grew and grew, so I sold to one of my drivers in 2003 to live by the seaside at Eastbourne in East Sussex. I bought a guest house, then a larger 28 bedroom hotel in partnership with a moron from California, writing a book called How Not to Run a Hotel. Financial hardship followed, I dealt in antiques and collectables and give talks on the subject to clubs and societies.

In 2012 I became the only person licensed by Eastbourne Borough Council to be a sight-seeing guide, and also take parties out on coaches for the day, giving commentaries. More on www. harrythewalker.com.

I am also a writer, hence this book, Buried Secrets. I won a writing competition some years ago, the prize was £100 plus a commission to write an erotic novel. That was called Hot Vegas. That caught the attention of an internet publisher, so I have a writing contract with them, the second book is called Hot Hits (it's about a contract hit lady). My third in the series is Hot Milf, that will be coming out some time soon.

There is also a short book called Volvo's Child, another longer one called Harry the Blogger, extracts from my daily blog. Then there is The Brick Monster, for children, all about a monster who is thrown out of the family cave because of his anti-social habits at the age of 57 (young for a monster).

If you are reading this and are employed in the funeral profession, I am quite sure that there will be sufficient material to be collated into More Buried Secrets. Why not contact me through my web site, or via email using harrythewriter@btinternet.com. I would love to hear from you.

I am also a public speaker. There are various topics, Buried Secrets; How Not to Run a Hotel; What's It Worth; Eastbourne History; The Royal Hippodrome Theatre. My fee is reasonable, and I am also booked as a keynote motivational speaker. The size of the audience is immaterial, I perform instead of coming out just with boring old dates and facts. Each talk is unique, I love to share my knowledge in an entertaining way.

Epilogue

What Else Do I Do Now?

I am a funeral celebrant. To those readers unaware, this means that I take funeral services, mainly at a crematorium, for families who don't necessarily require religious content. Someone who is a Humanist is strictly secular, but I see my role more as one that says the words on behalf of the family. I don't dictate, just ask what they want. So if they want the Lord's Prayer included, then that's fine by me, the same as Hymns.

When receiving instructions from the Funeral director, I contact the family, have a chat, introduce myself, while making an appointment to go round to see them. Quite often these days they require an order of service to be provided, so I discuss the content, what order everything is going to be said in, and also the music. This usually takes an hour, and I frequently have a cup of tea, as it creates a more relaxed atmosphere.

Why do funeral directors like to use me? Because I am old school, a safe pair of hands, because I liaise with them at all stages, so they don't have any nasty surprises. When I turn up to conduct the service, I have comprehensive notes, am on very good terms with the family, and am prepared for any eventuality. It makes such a difference, having that personal touch. It also makes such a difference to the funeral director, because they know that their family is in the hands of an experienced professional, one who doesn't get fazed if something out of the ordinary occurs. I anticipate problems, therefore they don't happen... *too often!*

You may also enjoy reading...

HOW NOT TO RUN A HOTEL

ESPECIALLY WHEN YOU REALISE THAT DEALING
WITH PEOPLE IS NOT YOUR STRONG POINT ...

BY **HARRY POPE**

Lightning Source UK Ltd.
Milton Keynes UK
UKHW01f1859260818
327839UK00001B/6/P